You Don't £1Million Cybersecurity Budget

Izak Oosthuizen

Prominence Publishing

www.prominencepublishing.com

The author can be reached as follows: communications@zhero.co.uk

You Don't Need a £1Million Cybersecurity Budget / Izak Oosthuizen. -- 1st ed.

ISBN: 978-1-990830-38-9

Acknowledgments

While I have drawn extensively on my own knowledge and experience in IT when writing *You Don't Need a £1 Million Cybersecurity Budget*, I would like to thank several individuals who have also made this project possible. Firstly, the four top-notch professionals who kindly agreed to be interviewed for the chapters on IoT, AI, Cyber Essentials, and Cyber Insurance. Respectively these are Professor Muttukrishnan Rajarajan, Director of the Centre for Cybersecurity at City, University of London, and Zhero's Head of Research and Development; Pranava Madhyastha, a Senior Lecturer in Computer Science at City, University of London; Simon Newman, the CEO of the Cyber Resilience Centre for London; and Roger Oldham, the Founder and Managing Director at London Market Forums and an experienced insurance industry adviser. Their invaluable insight and input, along with sound advice from Professor Ben Azvine, the Global Head of Security Research at BT, have taken the book to a whole new level.

I also extend my gratitude to my Zhero family, and two team members in particular, Anri du Toit and Chris Haverly. As Zhero's Head of Marketing and the Project Leader for the book, Anri's attention to detail, patience, and superb co-ordination skills, ensured that everything moved forward as planned and in a timely way. My thanks also go to Chris Haverly, Zhero's Content Writer and Researcher. Chris's thorough and current research will place *You Don't Need a £1 Million Cybersecurity Budget* in the mainstream, serving as an essential reference for SMEs wanting to strengthen their cybersecurity and cyber hygiene. I am also grateful to Suzanne Doyle-Ingram and her team at Prominence

Publishing for their planning, and editorial and design contributions. Last, and by no means least, I would like to thank my family. Annamaria, my wife, and my son, Zak, who have proven to be a source of untold support and inspiration.

Gratitude is also due to Zhero's clients – big and small, all having unique and diverse IT and cybersecurity requirements. By partnering with the likes of WeWork, Edmond de Rothschild, Giorgio Armani, and many businesses from all industry sectors, Zhero has become the powerhouse IT support and cybersecurity company it is today. When I founded Zhero in 2006, I could never have imagined that it would be one of the top 3% of IT support companies in the United Kingdom. This has been made possible through our clients, helping and shaping Zhero over the years.

My purpose in life is to help people by enabling them to solve their complex problems. They then have the freedom to work on what matters the most. As a man of faith and a grateful Christian, I consistently have hope for the future, always believing the best is ahead and genuinely believe that I can make a difference. I am blessed and honoured to be able to share my ideas on cybersecurity with the world. My prayer is that *You Don't Need a £1 Million Cybersecurity Budget* will be an all-important IT resource for SMEs, showing them the light at the end of their cybersecurity tunnel.

Table of Contents

Foreword

Cybersecurity remains centre stage in the business world today. Cybercriminals are neither selective nor discerning in whom they target. Most of the time, the media brings our attention to large-scale attacks on corporations and large organisations like the NHS, British Airways, and more recently, MGM Resorts. We seldom hear about attacks on small enterprises or SMEs. But they are not immune to cybercrime and are more likely to be preyed on.

Truth be told, SMEs are often caught between a rock and a hard place regarding their cybersecurity. They are often under-resourced and lack the financial clout of their big-league peers. Considering the current economic downturn, many SMEs are simply keeping their heads above water, believing that cybersecurity or cyber hygiene is unaffordable and out of reach.

Izak has been providing SMEs in the UK with cybersecurity and IT support for decades. He knows their pain points and the challenges they face when trying to maintain a secure network. He is also aware that many SMEs put cybersecurity education and training above all else. Unfortunately, this is something that will have little or no impact on curtailing cyber threats as human error will always be with us. Having seen and understood the IT challenges SMEs face, Izak offers security solutions that are designed to monitor and protect systems, reduce cybercrime overnight, and instil good cyber hygiene.

You Don't Need a £1 million Cybersecurity Budget is an invaluable tool for SMEs wanting to transform their cybersecurity. The book focuses on all the security issues that confound small businesses, including those with backups, inventory and assets, IT policy, email security, password management, and much more. The exponential market growth of AI and IoT has also opened up a can of worms, not only for cybersecurity but for data protection, privacy, and compliance. Using his keep-it-simple-and-straightforward approach, Izak takes readers on an in-depth cybersecurity journey, showing them how to eradicate threats by embracing the basics of IT security. You Don't Need a £1 million Cybersecurity Budget is a must-have for any SME wanting to secure its place in the digital future.

Prof. Ben Azvine PhD

Global Head of Security Research at BT

1

What Do We Do?

> "IT is not just another department in an organization. It's pervasive, like electricity."[1]
>
> – The Phoenix Project

The Phoenix Project may be a work of fiction about information technology and an unusual genre of literature, but no one can argue fact that IT, like electricity, is pervasive in almost every part of our lives. As such, IT security is not something that we can afford to be casual about. It always needs to be taken seriously, especially for businesses out there.

Unlike those born with the proverbial silver spoon in their mouths, I've had to work my way up in the world of IT and IT security. From humble beginnings, I've been in the business of IT services for twenty-five-plus years and have dedicated my career to keeping people safe and secure in the cybersecurity arena. That fact that cyber threats are far bigger than most people realize has been almost a sole motivation for this.

Cybercrime currently costs the world £6.4 trillion each year, equating to £150,000 every second. This is predicted to reach £8.4 trillion annually in the not-too-distant future, a sum greater than every economy in the world, bar the United States and China.[2] In dollar terms, amounting to

$10.5 trillion, this fortune marks the most significant shift of economic wealth in human history, poses a potential threat to incentives for innovation and investment, dwarfs the economic impact of natural disasters in a single year, and stands to generate more profit than the global trade of all major illegal drugs combined. With those terrifying statistics and facts in mind, it seems that work is cut out for my team and me.

The cybercrime landscape is only going to get worse, not better, as we head towards the next decade. Cisco tells us that there are already three times more networked devices on Earth than there are humans.[3] These could readily become easy pickings for the cybercriminals out there unless you have the best security and IT protection in place. To put this in perspective, let's read what some people have to say about the extent of cybercrime. In the words of former IBM CEO Ginni Rometty:

> "Cybercrime is the greatest threat to every company in the world."[4]

Warren Buffet took this one step further when he stressed that cyberattacks are the biggest threat we face, more problematic than nuclear weapons, a killer pandemic, or the worst natural disaster you can imagine.

Back to my humble beginnings in the world of information technology. I started Zhero, a London-based IT services and support company, in 2006. Then called Exe-Sys, my aim, along with that of my team, was to help micro-businesses and small and medium enterprises (SMEs) stay cyber-safe and guide them with best IT practices to protect their invaluable data and networks. At times, this has proven not to be the easiest of tasks, as effective cybersecurity can and does come with many challenges. Small operations like SMEs and those with fewer than ten employees are usually price-sensitive and under-resourced. More often than not, we have had to find the right balance between what works and what is practical, solutions that provide the minimum required security and that are within budget. Underlying this venture has always been our unwavering commitment as an IT service provider, essentially providing a comprehensive and time-tested IT insurance policy to our clients through our unlimited IT support model.

So, what do we do? Zhero's unlimited support model is wide-ranging and diverse, as you'll discover as you explore the chapters in this book. At this point, however, I'd like us to focus on critical aspects of security that we emphasise as cybersecurity solutions with our clients: Always on security with password policies, updates, systems inventory, monitoring, email security and comprehensive data backups. We've seen that when these cherry-picked cyber ingredients are aligned and adhered to, and when IT security is pervasive, SMEs and micros are free of the IT chaos that they would otherwise be forced to endure.

Malware has become a huge threat to the security of any digital system. And here's a jaw-dropping statistic if ever there was one - every day, 560,000 new pieces of malware are discovered and over 450,000 new malicious programs and potentially unwanted applications (PUA) are registered.[56] At the moment, over 1 billion malware programs exist on the planet.[7] With numbers like that, anybody who doesn't take their antivirus and anti-malware seriously is wearing light shoes for the long walk. Virus and malware monitoring needs to be 24/7, must be state of the art, and patched and updated in real-time. There are no other options. This is one of the basics that cannot be overlooked.

When it comes to antivirus and antimalware, it's vital to have an IT team that is highly knowledgeable and fully trained to offer all you best-in-class protection. You should also integrate your standard monitoring tools that will help you identify, block, and eliminate malware with negligible impact on the overall performance of the IT system. Ensure your protection is set in an aggressive mode to block all malware, even if it's zero-day. You should also standardise your protection and not have different anti-virus products. You should ensure that your protection is for both Windows and Mac devices. Contrary to common beliefs, Macs are not impervious to security risks. In fact, hackers have been progressively focusing on Mac users, seeking to capitalise on weaknesses to attain unauthorized entry into personal information, sensitive data, or even control over the device.

I believe that this kind of holistic approach to protection will ensure that you are always protected against cyberattacks. Many IT professionals might suggest using aggressive antivirus tools to immediately book anything that's potentially dodgy. I, personally, like to take virus security one step further, beyond the realm of malware. Some say that I go too far, but I know with antivirus protection enough is never enough. To my mind, antivirus and antimalware aren't enough to offer thorough protection. Neither are firewalls. It would be best if you also had dedicated anti-ransomware to give you an extra layer of protection. This will protect you should the ransomware find its way around the anti-virus. Time and time again, I've seen it as an additional fail-safe for businesses – the extra layer of protection they need against ransomware. And just as a reminder, ransomware is a type of malware that holds your data hostage and is only released when you pay a ransom. Ransomware is on the rise and is potentially the biggest cyber threat we will face in the foreseeable future. It is such a lucrative business for cybercriminals that one tool to protect yourself is not enough.

The first known ransomware attack reared its ugly head in 1989 with the attack on 20,000 AIDS researchers in 90 countries by Joseph Popp, Ph.D.[8] And the menace has been with us ever since. According to The Guardian, ransomware is "the defining cybercrime of the 2020s and hackers are only just beginning to exploit its potential to make money and sow mayhem."[9]

The information that I'm going to present will confirm these wise words. Who can forget the WannaCry attack of 2017, which targeted over 300,000 computers running on the Microsoft Windows operating system? The cryptoworm, which is still active, cost companies and organizations in 150 countries around the world an estimated $4 billion. The NHS (National Health Service) in England and FedEx were two of the worst hit.[10] Ransomware attacks grew exponentially during the pandemic. The 2020 attack on American software company, SolarWinds, affected more than 18,000 of its customers.[11] A year later, we saw the attack on Brazil-based meat processing company, JBS. The attack affected operations in the United States, Australia, Canada, and Brazil, and the company had no option but to pay the $11 million ransom in Bitcoin.[12] It goes without saying that ransomware is big business. So far, 246 ransomware attacks have plagued U.S. government departments at an estimated cost of $53 billion. Last year alone, ransomware cost the global economy billions of dollars, predicted to be $265 billion annually by 2031.[13]

On home soil, government authorities consider ransomware to be the biggest cyber threat in the UK. The CEO of the UK National Cyber Security Centre (NCSC) tells us:

> "Ransomware remains the biggest online threat to the UK and we are clear that organisations should not pay ransom demands. Cybersecurity is a collective effort and we urge the legal sector to help us tackle ransomware and keep the UK safe online."[14]

John Edwards, the UK Information Commissioner, added:

> "We've seen cybercrime costing UK firms billions over the last five years. The response to that must be vigilance, good cyber hygiene, including keeping appropriate backup files, and proper staff training to identify and stop attacks. Organisations will get more credit from those arrangements than by paying off the criminals."[15]

Back to my point about an added layer of protection against the ransomware menace. SMEs need something that will nip ransomware in the bud and prevent its infiltration into their IT networks. Something that works and is always on. Experience has taught me that ransomware often evades traditional antivirus software. You need a basic solution that knows what to look for and how to act accordingly. Any anti-ransomware technology you use should secure endpoints, firewalls, and servers and protect against local and remote unauthorized file encryption by malicious software. It has to go above and beyond built-in security software such as Microsoft Defender. Ideally, your anti-ransomware tools should work on Windows and Mac machines, offering real-time protection and 100% visibility across your entire network. Remember that ransomware attacks can hit at any time and come from anywhere. As a standard, your additional internet layer of ransomware protection will give you constant protection against phishing email attempts, insecure websites, malicious email attachments, and targeted attacks.

I could go on and on about the dangers of virus and ransomware, but I think that I've sufficiently spotlighted the need for ongoing protection against ransomware. So, let's move on to the next super key ingredient that should be at the forefront of all businesses for safeguarding - email security.

In many ways, email security fits in nicely with ransomware protection. It's important to understand that threats to our emails are one of the biggest of all and about 96% of all email is spam.[16] Email is used by almost everybody in an organization. It's also transmitted in an open format that can be read without decryption on almost any device. Emails also don't go directly from the sender to the recipient. Before landing in an inbox, they travel through different networks and servers, some of which may have vulnerabilities or be unsecured. Even if a user's workstation is secure, the network or server that emails travel through could easily be compromised. Talented bad actors can also access the metadata associated with emails, such as the subject, sender, recipient, attachments, and importance. If they do this, it's easy for them to impersonate a sender or manipulate email content. Put simply, the recipient receives an email that looks like it came from someone or somewhere it did not, something that we also call spoofing. Email is a primary instrument used by the bad guys for phishing and to spread ransomware. 83% of UK businesses that suffered a cyberattack in 2022 reported the attack type as phishing.[17]

Your IT team's security tools should prevent attack vectors such as phishing and spam from gaining unauthorised access to any part of your network. Again, your security must go beyond the likes of standard antivirus offerings that have been bundled with cloud services. As an aside, a recent report from the American technology firm, Cloudflare, tells us that Microsoft is the world's most impersonated brand used in phishing attacks. This is followed by the WHO (World Health Organisation), Google, SpaceX, and Salesforce.[18]

So, how do you ensure effective email security for your business? Always stay one step ahead of the bad guys – that's for sure. You should have a dedicated spam filter monitoring all emails around the clock and only deliver those from trusted sources to a user's inbox. A Secure Email Gateway (SEG) - essentially a firewall in the cloud between outsiders and user's email accounts - is a powerful tool that filters out potentially dangerous emails and users can later decide whether they want these to be delivered to their mailboxes or not. This decision is partially reliant on employee education and something you should invest in. Your employees will need to be trained to recognise attacks that are executed via email, such as social engineering and phishing. You should ensure best practice for your email security that includes antivirus protection where emails and attachments are screened for viruses. Users are then alerted if anything suspicious is detected.

Like most IT leaders, I am a stickler for password protocol. I must agree with what Bill Gates said at an RSA Security conference:

> "People use the same password on different systems, they write them down and they just don't meet the challenge for anything you really want to secure."[19]

That was way back in 2004, and it seems like nothing has changed. Passwords such as 654321, monkey, and qwerty are amongst the most popular passwords out there. According to a report, the most hacked password in the United States is indeed *password.*[20] And even worse, as Bill Gates confirms, people use the same password across multiple accounts and write them down in plain sight for all to see. None of that works for me.

For me, a rule of thumb when choosing a unique password is to find something easy to remember but hard to guess. That's not an easy task to begin with, especially since longer passwords with upper case letters, numbers, and special characters are much more difficult to crack. Nevertheless, when creating system login passwords, it is something that needs to be done. I am also an advocate of password managers also often referred to as a password vault. While they aren't suitable for system logins, they are invaluable for generating unique and complex passwords for each online account you have and are also stored in an encrypted vault. An added benefit is that password managers will automatically enter passwords into websites and apps, so users don't need to remember anything other than the email address associated with the account. You can also share passwords to other individuals in your business without revealing the actual password.

Good password policies mean more than simply choosing a complex password and using a password manager, and you should also ensure that multi-factor authentication (MFA) is enabled. For example, limiting login and password attempts and implementing a lock-out policy after several tries is great policy. Other examples are requiring users to change their primary password a few times each year, and enforcing password history so that a minimum number of unique passwords are used before a historical password can be used again. Ideally, a password should never be reused - not even a variation of an old password. Users also need to log out and lock their workstations before leaving them unsupervised. This also applies to logging out of portals and web browsers when you're not using them anymore. Always log out first - closing the program or window doesn't do the trick.

The next card in our deck is data backup. I know it's a cliché, but to me, backup is king. Judging from his statement made on World Backup Day, Rob Price at Snow Software agrees with me:

> "Banking collapse, volatile economies, pandemic and cybercrime don't change the fundamentals - data is the lifeblood of every organization and needs to be protected as such."[21]

In 2013, IBM declared that data was poised to become in the 21st century what steam power represented in the 18th, electricity in the 19th, and hydrocarbons in the 20th.[22] They were spot on. I don't think that nowadays there is a company that can function without data. A strategy that I recommend for resilient data backup is to apply the 3-2-1 rule. This means having three copies of your data on two different storage media and keeping one copy offsite. Backups must always be stored in a safe and secure place. It's also important to identify what data needs to be backed up and prioritise which data should be backed up more frequently and which data is business critical. Always ensure your backups are password-protected and encrypted.

Considering the proliferation of remote jobs and working from home in the workplace of today, cloud storage proves to be a viable solution for many of our clients. Software-as-a-Service (SaaS) offers both private and public cloud, with data backup and archive, cloud email and archive, and cloud security and protection. You may also be interested in a hybrid cloud environment that supports both local and remote data storage. I believe that backing up to the cloud is easy, convenient, affordable, and scalable. Cloud computing is an integral part of storage solutions today, providing flexibility and compatibility with existing environments and enabling SMEs and micros to plan for the future.

Cloud providers such as Google Drive, Microsoft One Drive, iCloud, and Dropbox make good choices for SMEs wanting online storage with a predictable and fixed monthly fee. You also pay less with annual *buy 10 get 2 free subscriptions.* These services also have encryption, so data remains secure while stored in the cloud. Again, we advise our clients not to make assumptions. Just because the third-party bears the name Microsoft or Apple, it doesn't mean that it's perfect. Data retrieval from the cloud is almost always slower than onsite data recovery. Don't assume that everything is being backed up by the third-party provider. Many companies only back up their data in the cloud, leaving mission-critical applications, such as Microsoft 365, Google Workspace, Salesforce.com, and Azure Active Directory, unprotected and vulnerable. Don't assume when the SaaS provider will do the backups. Just like with manual onsite backup, you'll need to check the integrity of those in the cloud. Remember that verified backups aren't real backups.

By following the simple rules, you will achieve – without any surprises - what Stephen Manley, CTO of the Californian software company Druva, strives for - self-driving backups. He says:

> "We have self-driving cars. It's time for self-driving backups. You need a solution that takes care of managing your backups, so you can spend your time working with the business."[23]

The last point I would like to mention in this glimpse into what we do is that system intrusion detection and intrusion prevention are must-haves. You can spend all the money in the world on cyber education and training, but one instance of human error is all it takes for a breach. Unfortunately, education and training will not turn the tide in the fight against cybercrime on their own. We shouldn't always be so quick to blame humans - everybody is prone to error at some point, you and I included. With 450,000 new forms of malware registered daily, education and training will not achieve the impossible. The only way to keep perpetrators at bay is to use appropriate and reliable technology and not depend on people. This is much more than using firewalls, making consistent backups, or regular updating. Ongoing IT monitoring and risk mitigation offer the best resilience and protection against cyber thieves. System and Compliance Manager, Daryl White says:

> "You can't hold firewalls and intrusion detection systems accountable. You can only hold people accountable."[24]

I disagree with White. If your car hasn't had a service or an MOT in five years, is it fair to blame the driver if it crashes? I think not. Yes, people make mistakes and will continue to make mistakes. That's human nature. What we need to ensure is that when somebody clicks on that suspicious link or downloads that unknown file, the story ends there.

While I always try to show businesses the light at the end of their cybersecurity and cyber hygiene tunnel, it's not always possible to take some of them through to the initial stage as many want to play by their own rules, rules that are suited to the way they operate. As I mentioned, we cherry-pick the best IT solutions to guarantee the minimum required security framework, essentially providing cybersecurity insurance. We simply can't provide this insurance if businesses want to remove anything from this cybersecurity wall - this includes anything from the basics like security updates to password policies. The risk lies in the basics. Unfortunately, sometimes we need to walk away from helping businesses to mitigate risks. Businesses need to remember that following the basics is critical, the rules same apply to a micro business with five team members, as to an enterprise with a thousand staff – there are no shortcuts. It doesn't matter if you do 90% of it right. It needs to be 100% on point.

2

What Do We See Out There?

> "If you put a key under the mat for the cops, a burglar can find it, too. Criminals are using every technology tool at their disposal to hack into people's accounts. If they know there's a key hidden somewhere, they won't stop until they find it."[1]
>
> – Tim Cook

I've started this chapter with some wise words from Apple's CEO for a very good reason. I see the 'key' that he is referring to as being analogous to the IT vulnerabilities and cybersecurity challenges that SMEs face. As you know, we do everything we can to safeguard the networks and data of small businesses under an unlimited insurance model with its many features including antivirus and malware, anti-ransomware, email security, password policies and data backup. Unfortunately - and I'm not scaremongering, despite all the warnings people like me in the IT security industry give them, many SMEs do leave their cyber keys under a mat, no matter how much security we put in place or how much cyber education and training their employees have. To me, IT security is like locking your house. It doesn't necessarily stop criminals, but if it's good enough, they'll move on to an easier target. Remember that 93% of data breaches can be avoided. Your system is as strong as your weakest link.

I often get asked, "What do you see out there?" And I provide an honest answer: Chaos and confusion. That may sound like a sweeping statement. However, this is the truth for many SMEs that don't follow the simple rules. The key is under the mat. The door is left unlocked. Cybersecurity vulnerabilities and challenges are profuse. IT systems are asking to be hacked. Anybody can become a victim and fall for some basic hacking techniques. It doesn't require much for cybercriminals to be successful.

I like to categorise these cyber challenges into two types - basic challenges and standard challenges. Basic cyber challenges are those for which an SME does not need much investment, and when adhered to, mean that most data breach can easily be avoided. The basics include IT policy, data backups, inventory, and systems access. The standard challenges may require a small investment but will be well within budget for most SMEs. The standard challenges we'll consider are network and systems management, email security, password policy, supplier due diligence, and dark web monitoring.

Let's look at the first of the basics - having an inadequate IT policy or not having one at all. IT security policies are wide-ranging and, as a bare minimum, should include acceptable use, change management, incident response, remote access procedures, vendor management, password creation and management, network security, data retention, Mobile Device Management (MDM), and Bring Your Own Device (BYOD) policies and procedures. Sadly, many of the SMEs that I have come across have lacked these critical security 101 components. The UK Department for Digital, Culture, Media & Sport tells us that only 35% of UK businesses use specific tools for security monitoring, o only a third carry out cybersecurity risk assessments, and even worse, only 14%

invest in threat intelligence.[2] Now take into account that SMEs, micros, large businesses, and corporates have all been lumped together for this analysis. Which of these pays more attention to cybersecurity? I think you know the answer, but just in case you need a clue, here's a recent statement made by the owner of an SME in the UK:

> "I think it's just… that we've known the word cybersecurity, but never thought, given the scale and size of our business, that it's something that we need to worry about. It's something that banks and government departments need to be concerned about in terms of data breaches. It's not something that is [a] concern for us."[3]

So, it seems that many SMEs think cybersecurity doesn't apply to them and that they don't need an IT policy. There are no rules governing network security, data management, and data protection. I've seen cases where contractors and freelancers are given access to sensitive company and client data from their devices. How on earth can you control what the contractor has on their machine? I've also been witness to a couple of horrifying cases where contractors, or even business owners, access company files from a shared, family computer at home.

What are the consequences of not having an IT security policy? The answer - CHAOS. Physical security policies are there to protect your physical assets like buildings, vehicles and equipment. IT security policies protect your data and your intellectual property (IP). IT equipment is home to sensitive data such as customer files and contact details. If the equipment is compromised, the data is exposed. What happens when that data falls into the wrong hands and you are not prepared? If you'd rather not find out, then your company needs an IT policy, whether it's a micro, an SME, a charity, or a large enterprise.

Now for the next basic challenge - data backups. You'll remember in Chapter 1 that Rob Price emphasized that data is the lifeblood of any company of any size.[4] I couldn't agree more. Backup is king! SMEs may be able to navigate through many of the IT challenges that they encounter, but without backups, they are lost in the wilderness. Here's something for a laugh:

"The server has been infected by ransomware."

"Oh, Dear! Where's the backup?"

"On the server."

Actually, it's not that funny! When data is gone, it's gone. In worse cases, I've seen companies that don't do backups. Or if they do, it's not according to best practices like the 3-2-1 rule, daily monitoring, multiple location storage, encryption, and password protection. We also see that some companies don't store data in central locations, and sometimes even the incorrect data is selected for the backups. Bruce Schneier tells us that while hardware may be easy to look after, data is a different story:

> "Hardware is easy to protect - lock it in a room, chain it to a desk, or buy a spare. Information poses more of a problem. It can exist in more than one place, be transported halfway across the planet in seconds, and be stolen without your knowledge."[5]

I also see those who are not in the know making assumptions about cloud storage. Just because data is in the cloud and managed by a third party, doesn't mean that it is backed up regularly or that backups are checked. SMEs need to take responsibility for the integrity of all their backups. This means that the cloud still needs to be backed up and have security updates applied. Never make assumptions that data is backed up. It needs to be checked and tested. Here are some key checks that we can make when it comes to backup. Is the backup an exact copy? What is the frequency of the backups? Does it work properly? Who has access to the backup? Do we have backups have encryption and password protection? Who is monitoring the backups and how often, daily? How often do we perform a restore tests? When you restore it to the test environment, can you access all your files as expected? How long will it take us to do a full data recovery? What will we use to restore our data to the server? Are we backing up the correct data after any system upgrades or changes? What is the retention of the backups, and how many versions do we have? Does my backup policy align with industry compliance requirements? Do we have any business-critical application data on local workstations that need to be part of the backups? Even if your cloud provider is making backups, it is essential to have an extra copy, taking us back to the 3-2-1 rule. To put it another way, only backing up with your cloud provider is like locking your keys inside your own car.

Data retention policies are often an afterthought or given no thought at all! Data retention is critical to information management. Without it, SMEs are showcasing their non-compliance with government and industry regulations. Storing data for too long is also problematic. This can result in operational inefficiencies, increased costs, such as storage costs, and legal and security risks. There's only one way to avoid these risks. That's to implement a data retention policy and stick to it. This makes data more accessible and safer and builds your customer trust.

The next cybersecurity thorn in the side for SMEs is inventory management. I've seen clients that simply have no control over their assets and not keeping proper inventory. They don't close the life cycle of any asset and leave them in a cupboard, not bothering to recycle by regulatory compliance. SMEs use unlicensed or free web-based software, software with illegal licenses costing a tenth of the price of the real deal, and sometimes even home editions, versions that are not meant to be used by businesses. I believe the bare minimum is to have a thorough knowledge of all installed software - what you have, the asset it is installed on, and who has access to it. And most important - is the software legal? The UK National Cyber Security Centre (NCSC) also tells us to be aware that unvetted software can spy on us. It has even raised concerns about Kaspersky, the Russian multinational cybersecurity and anti-virus provider headquartered in Moscow, Russia, and operated by a holding company in the UK.[6]

IT inventory management helps managers, and their teams, keep an eye on the assets they own, how they are behaving, and who is using them. Good inventory management means that you can pinpoint asset information and its associated data. You also save time and money in other ways. You can use your inventory management to gauge depreciation and see at a glance when assets and installed software are approaching end-of-life. Automating how you collect and manage data about your assets is much quicker than any manual process, giving you time to focus on your priorities.

It's also worth noting the importance of having a full inventory and monitoring of your network, such as internet routers, firewalls, switches, and the like. If you have an outrage, it will be much easier to identify the problem and take corrective steps. You'll get to the root cause of the problem a lot quicker. This is much more efficient than not having visibility on your network. I mean, what could be worse than not knowing where things are. If you don't know the physical location of a device on a network, how would you be able to fix the problem if your whole office has gone down? For example, there might be a switch hiding in the basement. If you don't have an inventory, you don't know about it, and it could take days to isolate the issue. The same applies to wireless access points. If one is located in the ceiling and you don't know where it is, how will you get the Wi-Fi up and running again if you go offline? So, the solution is simple – keep and inventory and monitor it.

I'm moving on to something that is an ongoing worry for businesses out there - administrative access and access control. And it doesn't matter if it is the store on the corner or Microsoft - access control is critical. Some companies have a policy of 'complete trust,' a free-for-all all to which everybody has administrative access. Users can install anything at any time. I don't think I need to elaborate on the cybersecurity risks of this approach.

What happens if somebody leaves or changes roles within a company? Often, they still have access to software and systems they don't need or use. Do they have access to confidential Human Resources data? What if a former employee has access to your cloud accounting package? This is the absolute chaos I have come across in my career. There must be a rigorous change process in place for these dangerous scenarios and regular internal access checks carried out as to who has access to what. Now's a suitable time to bring up the zero-trust approach to cybersecurity:

> "I have zero trust in you! I need to verify you first before I can trust you and grant access to the resource you want."[7]

Bringing the point home, this means that you should never trust and always verify. It doesn't matter where people are working from and how they are accessing resources. Zero trust architecture means reinforcing and securing your cybersecurity perimeter and only giving access to those who need it, when they need it.

Here are some more of the basic challenges that we face when dealing with SMEs. Some of them use expired software with no antivirus or have no set standards for software management and control, mixing and matching free and trial versions of programs. I've seen cases where SMEs have no protocol or standard for enforcing security updates, meaning systems are out of date and completely exposed to attacks. Even worse, sometimes assets have not been updated for years. Due to the lack of resources or expertise, workstations are not properly set up and are not connected to a central system that is managing user's access and passwords. I've seen users log into a PC or Mac with a shared password, sometimes even worse by setting up without a password. For some strange reason, many believe that Macs are secure and impenetrable. They're not. While Macs may not be as commonly targeted by cybercriminals as Microsoft's Windows platform, they are not immune to attacks. A recent example involved a mysterious malware called Silver Sparrow, which specifically aimed at the new M1 Macs, compromising as many as 30,000 Apple computers.[8] This all goes back to what I said earlier about having a decent IT security policy. Also, ensure that your Mac has anti-virus and anti-ransomware protection – the game hasn't changed, and the rules remain the same. You always need multilevel defence.

Now that we've covered the basic challenges, let's take a look at a few of the standard challenges and vulnerabilities that I've observed when working with SMEs. The first of these is ineffective network management and the use of outdated systems. Sometimes, it's more than inadequate management - IT networks aren't managed at all. Often, these businesses claim that they don't have the money for ongoing support and can only afford the reactive break-fix model of IT services and support. This is a big mistake. With digital transformation increasingly shaping the way we work and do business, everybody needs an optimised IT infrastructure, a stable network, and a guaranteed response and repair time. I'd also like to point out a major problem with the break-fix model and that is the assumption of responsibility. Who is really responsible? It's a bit of a dilemma, as the IT supplier will think the owner is responsible. The owner will think that the onus is on the IT supplier.

Another observation that has almost given me grey hair overnight is the use of default passwords on network equipment such as routers, switches, access points, and Internet of Things (IoT) devices. Think of the analogy of selling a house. If somebody buys your home but never changes the locks, what then? Easy answer: your keys can always be used for access. The issue with network equipment is that everyone has a copy of the key, not only the previous owner. The same applies to network equipment. If you never change the password, anybody who knows it can access the network. Those who don't change default passwords are asking for trouble, as default settings provide an easy attack vector for cybercrooks. Put simply, attackers can almost effortlessly obtain these logins and access the devices on your network - usually with admin rights. If that happens, your network can be taken over, and your data will be in the wrong hands. When you consider that up to 80% of successful data breaches are caused by compromised passwords, you can understand the need to change from defaults to unique login credentials.[9]

What about using outdated systems and software? Take servers and firewalls, for example. Using old technology with inadequate protection increases vulnerability to ransomware attacks. Also, they tend to have unpatched security vulnerabilities and are an easy target for the bad guys out there. As with any legacy devices, vendors stop providing support and updates, and devices remain unpatched. Besides these cybersecurity concerns, old servers and firewalls are prone to crashing, which leads to system downtime. They are much less efficient than their newer counterparts, have lower performance capabilities, and can be more expensive to maintain. It's also very common that when you are using older servers, you often need to wing it to make it compatible with the network. You almost have to reverse-engineer the software to get things working. In essence, you are not capitalising on the potential of your software.

So why do SMEs hold on to these outmoded machines? They claim to save money. The fact of the matter is that maintaining and trouble-shooting outdated firewalls and servers is usually more costly than upgrading to modern tech. My motto here is "Out with the old, in with the new." It's important to see this as an investment in your security. My view is supported by the White House Cybersecurity Advisor, Richard Clarke:

> "If you spend more on coffee than on IT security, you will be hacked. What's more, you deserve to be hacked."[10]

Much of the same applies to SMEs using outdated operating systems and software reaching end-of-life. For example, Microsoft 365 apps are no longer supported on Windows 7, Windows 8, or Windows 8.1 now that these operating systems have reached their end-of-support dates. Besides a lack of vendor support, using outdated operating systems will question compliance with regulations and standards, such as GDPR (the European Union General Data Protection Regulation), and increase vulnerability to cyberattacks and hence increase legal liability. Any SME using an outdated OS will have doubt cast over its ability to meet industry standards and best cybersecurity practices and data privacy. When this is discovered, reputational damage follows, and customers look for alternative suppliers. For SMEs working in regulated industries like finance or healthcare, failure to meet industry standards could have legal consequences. Vendors, partners, and customers usually expect SMEs to use up-to-date software and hardware. Not doing this is a breach of contract, also resulting in legal action. I have seen this and worse happening to small businesses that do not stick to the simple rules.

In the worst case, some businesses decide to conceal a breach, thinking that it will go unnoticed. These things never do. Before the exposure of a breach, there is normally a discovery phase in which the compromise is investigated. CEOs might think that they can hide it and get away with it, but it's just a matter of time. Forensic investigation almost always leads to exposure. Concealing a breach can be very costly, indeed, including GDPR fines and severe reputational damage.

The next standard challenge facing SMEs, and a major bugbear of mine, is email security, or the lack thereof. Remember that email is a primary tool used in phishing and ransomware attacks. 3.4 billion phishing emails are sent every day, and a ransomware or phishing attack happens every 11 seconds. Added to this, breaches caused by phishing can take up to 295 days or more to identify and contain.[11] Do SMEs take heed of these statistics? I know some that don't. They don't have email and data retention setup, altogether an alarming breach of regulatory compliance. Moreover, I've observed two users at a company - I won't mention the name - share Microsoft Outlook and Teams credentials so one of them could access files while the other was on the road without internet access. Talk about a breach of the company IT policy and GDPR, not to mention the risks that the users were exposing themselves to.

I've also been privy to email systems that have had some degree of security but have anti-spam solutions missing. Again, this is a major cybersecurity concern, given the number of spam messages landing in email accounts every day. Every account needs filtering, and companies should consider this as a prerequisite to good cybersecurity and cyber hygiene. Filtering ensures that spam, viruses, and malware are detected before they reach a user. Reliable anti-spam software uses filters that only allow emails from known and approved email addresses to access user inboxes.

As a brief aside, somebody once asked me what happens if they open a spam email accidentally. Will their computer or the network get infected? In short, the answer is no. Your data can't be compromised simply by opening a phishing email. Nevertheless, hackers can still harvest data about you and use this to devise more targeted attacks against you. For those who are tempted to open spam just for a look-see, I say thread carefully - curiosity killed the cat after all. That said, if somebody should accidentally click on a harmful email, one would hope that the rest of the system would be compliant and protect you.

Education and training are one way of getting your team up to speed with email security. With awareness training, which I believe is super important, many errors and bad practices when using email and the web can be avoided. It's a bit like making a fledging vehicle driver aware of road signs, and to watch out for sharp turns in a road or a wet and slippery surface. Warnings are only precautionary – they don't mitigate the risk. So, going back to what I mentioned in the previous chapter, no amount of training will negate a single mistake made by a human. One instance of human error is all it takes for a breach. Here are some rather unkind, and not necessarily true, words from Mike Danseglio, a program manager at Microsoft Security Solutions:

> "Phishing is a major problem because there really is no patch for human stupidity."[12]

Yes, people make foolish decisions, including when they act without thinking. But I will reiterate what I said in Chapter 1 - blaming people for human error and calling them stupid is not a cybersecurity solution. Protecting technology with technology is the only way that you can keep the key under the mat and out of the hands of hackers.

Along with a lack of adherence to email security, my other pet hate is users' lack of respect for strong passwords and password policies - if they even exist. I cannot count the number of times that I've seen users sending usernames and passwords in the same email message, not using password managers or vaults, and using Post-it notes as a trigger to remember passwords. To my mind, every user should have this slogan in plain sight of their workstation:

> "Passwords are like toothbrushes. They are best when new and should never be shared."[13]

I do believe that the responsibility for good password practice is beyond the realm of single users. It is management who should develop a robust password policy, implement it, and ensure that team players stick to it. Bear in mind that creating an IT security policy or password policy in itself doesn't guarantee security. Do speed limits deter speeding drivers? I think not.

In my 25 years in IT, I've also experienced situations where SMEs do not carry out supplier due diligence. If a supplier handles sensitive data - especially customer data - it is an absolute must to check what security they have in place. Companies that practise good due diligence have better visibility of their supply chain and can identify any security issues that might make one of their suppliers open to a breach. SMEs that ignore this crucial aspect of cybersecurity could easily experience a supply chain attack and end up like SolarWinds or Kaseya.

Kaseya, an IT solutions developer for MSPs and enterprise clients, became a victim of a cyberattack in July 2021. A vulnerability in its security resulted in an estimated 1,500 of its clients getting infected by ransomware, causing widespread downtime. The attacks multiplied before Kaseya could warn everyone, rapidly encrypting data and demanding ransoms of as much as $5 million per victim.[14] These were Managed Service Providers (MSPs), all tasked with the duty of looking after the data of their clients. Victor Gevers, head of the Dutch Institute for Vulnerability Disclosure, had warned Kaseya before the incident and later said:

> "Now that criminals see how powerful MSP attacks can be, they are already busy, they have already moved on, and we don't know where. This is going to happen again and again."[15]

Mobile Device Management (MDM) is another area of concern for SMEs, especially with the increase in BYOD, remote working, and working from home. Without an MDM policy, anybody can access business email and data from any mobile phone, which the average hacker could have access to. How do you know if a mobile phone has not been jailbroken? What software might be spying on the mobile essentially gaining access to sensitive data? This is just like the contractors I mentioned using their own devices to access sensitive corporate data. MDM is often available at no extra charge and simply needs to be setup, configured and implemented.

Monitoring the Dark Web is another thing that is missing for the SME IT bundle. This is something that shouldn't be ignored, and it is vital to check for any past breaches on platforms, apps, or online software that users access. A proactive approach is to have real-time monitoring so that any potential vulnerabilities can be instantly detected and flagged. Dark Web monitoring will also help in the worst-case scenario. It provides a much faster incident response time should your precious data end up in the hands of cybercriminals. You will then be able to reduce the overall window of opportunity that these guys have to make copies of the data and try to sell it on the Dark Web.

Owners of SMEs are often taken in by trends in the cyberspace community, especially with the media's leverage of scare tactics, human emotions, and gullibility. One minute, people are obsessed with the Dark Web, and the next it's all about incident response, and then biometrics. Then those are forgotten, and suddenly, the focal point is effective password management. The building blocks of cybersecurity are interdependent. One component relies on another. You can't apply a shopping basket approach to cybersecurity. You need all the basic components. Always.

Another big problem is that owners of SMEs often dominate the rules and govern how their IT is managed. Many IT providers aren't willing to walk away for fear of losing a precious client. As such, they enable misconfigurations and dubious setups. Worse still, is business owners or office managers "DYI'ing" their IT. We need to find a way to relegate and have true visibility on how all systems and networks are configured.

We need a technical framework to follow like a "Minimum Required Framework." This framework should provide complete visibility over password policies, connected systems and used for, single sign-on (SSO) emails, workstations and files, VPN, and cloud monitoring and backups. The Minimum Required Framework means that networks are monitored around the clock and security updates are always applied. Antivirus guarantees endpoint detection and response (EDR), identifying security breaches as they happen and facilitating rapid response and mitigation. When fully integrated into any IT network, the "Minimum Required Framework" provides businesses with peace of mind knowing that they have fully managed data protection in place.

This is the kind of solution you should be looking for to keep your hardware, software, and data secure.

In this chapter, I have painted a dismal picture of the cybersecurity practices and cyber hygiene of SMEs. Yes, there are SMEs operating within the boundaries of safety and security. But sadly, the reality is that most of them do break the rules. I have simply used this opportunity to provide a summary of bad practices – and sometimes dangerously bad – that I have observed and noted through the years. Unfortunately, that's what we see out there. Let's end here with some wisdom from Eugene Howard Spafford, aka Spaf, an American professor of computer science at Purdue University. Reflecting upon the basic and standard cybersecurity challenges that some SMEs face, I echo his sentiments:

"Those of us in security are very much like heart doctors - cardiologists. Our patients know that lack of exercise, too much dietary fat, and smoking are all bad for them. But they will continue to smoke, eat fried foods, and practice being couch potatoes until they have their infarction. Then they want a magic pill to make them better all at once, without the effort. And by the way, they claim loudly that their condition really isn't their fault - it was genetics, or the tobacco companies, or McDonalds that was to blame. And they blame us for not taking better care of them. Does this sound familiar? But it doesn't have to be this way. We can do things better. We need to stop doing business as usual and start focusing on end-to-end quality. Security needs to be built in from the start - not slapped on after the fact."[16]

I believe that cybersecurity is like a wall with many bricks. When all the bricks are aligned and where they should be, everything works perfectly. If one brick is missing, you are exposed, and the wall will collapse. To keep the wall intact and invulnerable, all you need to do is stick to the basics. As I said earlier, these basics are like the annual MOT for your car. If we can ensure and control that businesses have them in place, over 95% of cyber risk is permanently removed and gone for good for most SMEs.

3

Stick to the Simple Rules! - KISS

> "One single vulnerability is all an attacker needs."[1]

Those profound words come from the mouth of Window Snyder, the American IT expert who has had senior cybersecurity roles at corporates like Microsoft, Apple, Fastly, Intel, and Mozilla.[2] Like Snyder, I'm well aware that almost any device or network is hackable - that's no secret.

With his words in mind, I'd also like to reflect on an incident from many years ago – something that will stick with me for life. We were working at a prestigious London-based hedge fund doing the installation for the owner. In a very patronising and calm way, he shouted across the office at one of my engineers – KISS! Afterwards, we were talking about it internally, grasping what he had said. His simple words gave me direction on how to manage IT in the future. When you first hear it, 'keep it simple and stupid' is not the best news you want to digest. However, that is one of the fundamental things about successful IT and keeping hackers at bay – keep everything as simple as possible. That way, we remove the risks of "one single vulnerability." Simplicity is best, so keep a simple standard.

Attacks happen in seconds but often go undetected for months. All the while, the bad guys are harvesting data and further infiltrating systems.

It's the scale of hacking that really worries me, as hackers are relentless in their endeavours to cripple systems and make money. The UK Government has estimated that there were about 2.39 million instances of cybercrime and approximately 49,000 instances of fraud in the last twelve months.[3] Also, as I mentioned in Chapter 1, businesses and individuals pay a high price for cybercrime, currently standing at £6.4 trillion each year.[4] While downtime and paying ransoms may be digestible for corporates, for SMEs and micro-enterprises, a single incident can lead to them shutting shop. It's been reported that 60% of SMEs go burst within six months of being victims of a cyberattack or data breach.

To my dismay, some SMEs don't take these warning signs seriously or don't even acknowledge them. They treat cyber hygiene and appropriate cybersecurity as if they were elephants in the room, an afterthought or an annoyance. But I reiterate - good cyber hygiene and cybersecurity strategies are affordable, manageable, and well within the operational scope of SMEs. In this chapter, I'm going to delve deeper into what small businesses can do to avoid being hacked. Moreover, if the worst comes to the worst, I would like SMEs to take comfort in knowing that being hacked doesn't mean the end of the road for the business. Recognising the signs of a hack can potentially nip it in the bud and avoid the breach going undetected for months on end. SMEs will also be empowered and feel confident when they know what steps to take during a hack. Before getting into all of that, let's continue to explore probably the biggest cyber threat out there and my pet hate: ransomware.

It's estimated that each year there are about 600 million global ransomware attacks, accounting for 20% of all breaches.[5] That's a huge number! In the UK, a third of the businesses hit by ransomware attacks lose revenue, and 20% are forced to close shop.[6] The attacks vary in severity and impact, but, as we all know, the one at the top of the heap is the WannaCry incident of 2017. As a reminder, this high-profile attack took down more than 200,000 computers in over 150 countries. The hackers encrypted data on the infected devices and demanded $300 in Bitcoin per user to prevent having their data deleted. Global damages resulting from the attack are estimated at $4 billion. In the UK, The National Health Service (NHS) was forced to cancel 19,000 appointments at a cost of £92 million.[7] This is what the NHS had to say about WannaCry after the event:

> "A relatively unsophisticated attack and could have been prevented by following basic IT security best practice."[8]

But what was WannaCry ransomware? Put simply, WannaCry was malicious software that took advantage of vulnerabilities in unpatched Microsoft Windows operating systems. Before the WannaCry attack, the vulnerability known as *Eternal Blue* was exposed by the hacking group *The Shadow Brokers*. Rumour has it that *Eternal Blue* was developed by the United States National Security Agency (NSA). Once discovered, Microsoft quickly released a patch to remove the vulnerability. However, people being as they are, ignored the update, either through lack of awareness or education. So, these questions remain - How could the risk have been mitigated? In general, to what extent can cyberattacks be attributed to human error or insider threats? What can we do to put an end to these attacks altogether?

You should also bear in mind that what hackers can get out of SMEs is small potatoes compared to lucrative attacks on wealthy corporations.

That's why the media only tells us about the large-scale hacks on the likes of the NHS, SolarWinds, Kaseya, and Colonial Pipeline. SMEs and microenterprises aren't in that league, and typically, advanced attacks don't apply to them. For the average hacker, day-to-day attempts to break into systems are easy to do.

A good example is the August 2023 attack on CloudNordic, a Danish cloud solutions and enterprise hosting for many SMEs. The self-proclaimed "Nordic cloud experts" suffered a ransomware attack, claiming that the infection happened when servers were being moved from one data centre to another. The ransomware paralyzed all its systems and wiped both the company and customers' websites and email systems. Even backups were held hostage. CloudNordic told its customers to consider all their data lost forever. In an online forum, the company admitted:

> "We cannot and do not want to meet the financial demands of the criminal hackers for ransom. Unfortunately, it has proved impossible to recreate more data, and the majority of our customers have thus lost all data with us."[9]

SMEs must secure their endpoints and deploy all the basic building blocks of cybersecurity. Otherwise, they face the risk of being hacked, just like CloudNordic. Remember that sadly – and I repeat the sad part of it, CloudNordic lost all their backups because they were stored on the same network. Maybe they should have applied the 3-2-1 backup rule. But it's too late now. That said, let's look at how we can identify the signs of hacking.

The NCSC (National Cyber Security Centre) and NCA (National Crime Agency) recently reported that ransomware continues to thrive in the UK while cyber hygiene and cybersecurity remain lax.[10] I'm sure that SMEs are included in this revelation. The same white paper tells us that both ransomware and extortion attacks have increased exponentially since 2017. NCSC CEO, Lindy Cameron comments:

> "Since IT systems are now ubiquitous, ransomware attacks can be truly devastating for victims and their customers, which is why it remains the most acute cyber threat for most UK businesses and organisations. Attacks can affect every aspect of an organisation's operation, hitting finances, compromising customer data, disrupting operational delivery, eroding trust and damaging reputations. The impact will be felt in the short and long term, particularly when organisations are unprepared. Recovery is often lengthy and costly."[11]

Cameron really brings home the ugly truth about what ransomware is capable of. As she says, recovery from a ransomware attack - if at all possible - is not a quick fix. It's an expensive and time-consuming process from which some SMEs may never fully recover. Companies that have breached data will also be under scrutiny by data protection authorities such as the ICO (Information Commissioners Office) and may end up paying huge fines for UK GDPR non-compliance. Again, we may be able to recover from backups but one question still remains. What about the reputational loss and potential fines you might face regardless of recovery?

What is even more alarming is the extent to which the ransomware ecosystem has specialized. So, forget SaaS, PaaS, IaaS, DRaaS, and all the other services. Now we have RaaS (Ransomware-as-a-Service), along with online marketplaces and forums, and easy-to-use cybercrime tools, including AI. This is almost unbelievable. You can buy RaaS software as a tool that will hold software, and by extension, a company to ransom. These have all lowered the barriers to entry for the average cybercriminal, making it much easier to carry out an attack. Organized crime, in pursuit of "big game hunting," has evolved from attacking the network of a small organization or single user, although these, of course, continue to happen daily. Damaging the network of a large enterprise means that cybercriminals can demand higher payments, and their ROI is that much bigger.

I am also dumbstruck by the scale of operation of these guys. OCGs (organized crime groups), such as Evil Corp, comprise highly organized and skilled criminal hackers operating much like legitimate businesses with offices, salaries, holiday and sick pay, and other benefits.[12] The biggest cyber threat to the UK comes from the likes of Russian-speaking OCGs such as Evil Corp. They have helped shape the ransomware landscape by offering RaaS on marketplaces and making this form of cybercrime much more accessible and scalable. Many of these marketplaces are similar to automated vending carts (AVCs) and allow criminals to buy credentials, typically under $100 for most services.

I'm also not surprised that the NCSC and NCA reveal that most of the initial accesses by ransomware are not targeted against a particular organization or industry sector. These bad actors are really only interested in one thing - money. So, penetration is opportunistic rather than targeted. Cybercriminals will buy accesses that look appealing and profitable or will look for vulnerabilities in software and devices often used on IT networks, those of SMEs included. Devices also include Microsoft Exchange servers that are unpatched. The NCSC also believes that the majority of ransomware incidents are not due to sophisticated attack techniques but are usually the result of poor cyber hygiene.[13] As we all know, poor cyber hygiene can include anything from poor password protection and management, not patching your devices, and lack of MFA. Not having MFA provides cybercriminals with an open door to your data, and this is why many ransomware attacks are successful.

I'd like to share another recent case of a ransomware attack that could have easily been avoided. MGM Resorts, a company with a market cap of approximately $13 billion as of October 2023, operates hundreds of hotel and gaming establishments across the globe, with a prominent presence in Las Vegas. On 11 September 2023, three days after acknowledging a significant cyberattack, one of the largest hospitality outfits in the United States, still grappled with paralyzed hotel booking systems and casino slot machines. MGM's casinos remained out of action for four days, with large queues forming as staff resorted to relying on pen and paper. Guests also reported that TV services were down in hotel rooms, along with MGM's phone lines. This cyber incident took a toll on MGM Resorts, resulting in a more than 6% decline in its share price.[14] Insider sources claim a hacking group known as *Scattered Spider* is believed to be responsible for the attack. The FBI is actively investigating the matter.

The attack is said to be a social engineering kind of vishing attack. The attacker pretended to be a person working in MGM, impersonating somebody they found on LinkedIn. They called the help desk and made help desk reset the password belonging to that person. Afterward, using the credentials, they penetrated the system, encrypted or stole critical data, and informed the related people about what they did or had. This attack could have been avoided with better authentication protocols, which would have allowed the service desk to verify that the "locked out employee" was not who they claimed to be. If there is an authorization process in your infrastructure that is not automated already, you should be much more alert or have a plan to automate it. You cannot trust people or systems - trust and security do not coexist. If you want to achieve real security, there needs to be zero trust.

The MGM attack could have been avoided by applying the MFA approach. For example, a code is only texted to a number that is on the system. Another very simple mistake I believe is that you should never use your primary credentials, such as those used daily for email, to have elevated access to other systems. This is an exceptionally poor password management protocol, along with inadequate elevated credential management. At all times, businesses should ensure that there is a demarcation between the day-to-day credentials and those for elevated and privileged access – essentially the credentials that have administrative access.

Analysts believe MGM Resorts International was losing between $4.2 million and $8.4 million in daily revenue or between 10% and 20%.[15] As yet, the company has not acknowledged making any ransom payments to the hackers. MGM's insurance technology team calculated that a ransom could cost between $30 million and $50 million. The company is covered by a $200 million cyber insurance policy covering ransom payments and business interruption.[16]

The MGM incident follows hot on the heels of the attack on Caesars Entertainment, the largest U.S. casino chain with the most extensive loyalty program in the industry. On 7 September 2023, attackers stole its loyalty program database, which stores driver's license numbers and social security numbers for many customers. Caesars paid the ransom of roughly $15 million, half of the attackers' initial $30 million demand, in order to avoid the threat of triple extortion.[17]

My good friend, Professor Ben Azvinc, the Global Head of Security Research at BT, also tells me that more than 50% of malicious attacks are not picked up by threat monitoring tools and that 53% of enterprise security leaders don't know if their cybersecurity tools are working. Added to what I said earlier, Ben also confirms that it takes a company about seven months to identify a breach. Things have certainly come a long way since the birth of computer viruses in the 1990s. We now live in a world of autonomous malware constantly threatening supply chain attacks.

In my opinion, many of these threat monitoring tools that we see out there today, are reactive in nature, and are also expensive. If the systems are set up correctly and with a simplified approach, it wouldn't matter if threat indicators were positive or negative. You would still be protected, regardless. This will also save people from spending endless hours analysing data which doesn't say much. All it tells us is that we are reactive and don't follow a simplified approach. Quick-fix, reactive solutions are not solutions at all.

I know that I've painted a grim picture of ransomware and the consequences of an attack, but how will you know if your computer is under attack from ransomware or anything else? One sure way that you'll know is the appearance of random messages and popups telling you that your device has been infected. In all likelihood, these communications will have a *Remove Virus* or *Clean Your PC* button. Click on it, and guess what? You've downloaded malware onto your computer. Along similar lines are fake protection alerts. Phishers use these to gain access to an administrator's accounts. For example, fake Office 365 alerts may claim that a licence has expired and that users must log in to check payment information. Remember that these fake viruses are simply using scare tactics. They display a warning of non-existent threats with the intention of making you panic. Their modus operandi? Getting you to click and pay to eliminate the imaginary threat.

When you start receiving spoofing emails, that's another sure sign that you've been hacked. The main reason behind spoofing is to launch phishing attacks. Emails appear to be from your bank, employer, or online sellers like Amazon. Spoofing emails are particularly dangerous because the recipient thinks they are from a trusted sender. Spoof emails are also unlikely to get blocked by spam filters, and the body of the email often looks just like that you'd receive from the trusted sender. The intentions of spoofing hackers include stealing your account credentials, deploying ransomware, or even using your identity to open fraudulent accounts. Spoofed emails often also contain trojans, fake software loaded with malware, and other viruses. Robust email security is critical. You need to ensure that your public-facing naming, aka domain naming system (DNS), is set up securely and correctly. None of this well break the bank.

What's next in the delightful world of hackers and hacking? Hackers also find ways of delivering malware by installing unwanted toolbars, add-ons, and extensions. The most well-known and notorious of these is *Ask*, a toolbar that changes your browser homepage like Google or Firefox and replaces your default search engine without your permission. Unwanted toolbars are both pesky and dangerous, spamming you with ads, tracking your browsing history, or hijacking your browser settings like Ask does. Mac owners should also be wary. Safari is also vulnerable to this kind of hacking, and users may need to reset the browser to remove unwanted toolbars.

Likened to unwanted toolbars and spoofing email, but potentially more of a threat is unknown software. Unknown software can easily be installed on your device by clicking on a suspicious-looking link or downloading unknown files from a website or email attachment. Hackers use the software for phishing, ransomware, installing trojans, and activating malware. Unwanted software can also result in your machine becoming infected with spyware, which can surreptitiously collect personal data such as passwords, pins, payment information, and private messages. A scary example of spyware is DarkHotel, operated by a South Korean advanced persistent threat (APT) group. DarkHotel targets business and government leaders using unsecured public Wi-Fi in hotels. For example, after checking in to his 5-star accommodation for the night, one guest tried to get online. As he was signing into the hotel network, he got a pop-up alerting him to an Adobe update. He accepted the download, and spyware was installed on his computer, giving sophisticated attackers access to the hotel's IT system and all the data contained therein. The hospitality sector is particularly vulnerable to this type of cyber espionage.

Malicious redirects are another trick that hackers have up their sleeves. This common attack is where a user is directed from a legitimate website to another site. The intention is usually to generate advertising impressions. Malicious redirects can also exploit vulnerabilities and install malware on your device. Attackers often use WordPress websites as an entry point to plant redirect code, usually JavaScript. Malicious redirects do get picked up by search engines, and infected websites are blacklisted. Even when the redirect is removed, it can be tricky and expensive to convince Google to unflag your site and allow its ranking to slowly be restored.

Social media invitations and social engineering is another issue facing us all. A typical symptom of social media hacking is when your friend receives invites or messages from you - communications that you never sent. Large-scale hacks of social media platforms can cause huge data loss, massive financial loss, identity theft, and the viral spread of malicious content. Social media hacks rank among some of the worst of them all. Taking the top spot is the Yahoo breach of 2013, where the accounts of 3 billion users were exposed. The LinkedIn Dark Web breach in June 2021 exposed selected information of its entire 700 million customer base. In April 2019, 530 million Facebook users were hacked, including phone numbers, account names, and Facebook IDs. Dubsmash, MySpace, and the Chinese social media site Weibo have also been victims of social engineering.[18] And here's a word to the wise from John McAfee:

> "Social engineering has become about 75% of an average hacker's toolkit, and for the most successful hackers, it reaches 90% or more."[19]

A sure sign of knowing you've been hacked is when your online passwords don't work. Hackers typically use social engineering, key-stroke logging, and network analysers to crack passwords, access accounts, and change passwords. Also among the favourites are brute force attacks and man-in-the-middle attacks. These terms may sound fancy and intimidating, but again if we just go back to the basics of healthy password and credential management, they are nothing more than scaremongering phraseology. Yes, 'brute force' does sound scary but there is nothing to fear when you use a password vault and have all the simple controls in place.

So, what has happened if you are unable to access your files? It's likely that your device has been infected with ransomware, either downloaded from attachments in phishing emails or installations from infected websites. But don't worry, you'll hear from the bad guys soon enough. They know that you want your data back and that you are willing to pay for that privilege. After encrypting your files, they'll send you that inevitable ransom demand, either in a window, an app, or a full-screen message.

Some folks have asked me what to do if they get hacked. My response is to fight back! Yes, you need to take charge of the situation and apply some damage control. Firstly, you may not be sure of the source or location of the attack, especially if you are using a centralised network. Start by securing your systems and isolating devices from the network. You can change permissions and limit access to shared files, applications, and programs. In the worst case scenario of encryption, one way to stop ransomware is to prevent users from having access. This way, they can't make any changes to files and folders. If possible, disconnect from the internet. Even if only for a short while, it'll mean that attackers can't do any more damage than they've already done. This insight from neuroscientist Abhijit Naskar should help us all understand why going offline is essential:

> "No technology that's connected to the Internet is unhackable."[20]

Then, I would recommend doing a total scan. Run a full antivirus and malware scan on every network computer and mobile endpoint. In this way, you'll quickly isolate infected devices. I would also take an inventory and review all of your network applications and those installed on individual machines. This shouldn't be an issue if you have good cyber hygiene in place, but if any app appears to come from an illegitimate vendor or developer, uninstall it immediately. I would also question how it was installed onto your network in the first place. In addition, make sure that your critical security patches are up to date and that your security software is updated in real time.

Next comes lockdown. During a hack, or even if you just suspect you've been hacked, locking down your accounts is critical. Change all the passwords to your online accounts, especially those providing access to sensitive information or financial transactions. You will need to change user logins to access your network. Secure your Wi-Fi by changing the wireless password. Finally, don't keep it to yourself. You'll need your team's support to get you through the crisis.

If your home computer has been hacked, tell your family and friends. It's a good idea for them to delete any suspicious-looking emails or social media messages that appear to be sent by you. Remember, one single vulnerability is all an attacker needs. You know it, and so should those who are closest to you. If you are uncertain about the root cause of the problem, make an immediate backup of the current state of your data. This is an extra precaution in case any of your other isolation methods are doing further damage.

Recognising that you've been hacked and doing damage control is all remedial. What you should be asking is how to avoid being hacked in the first place. Start by thinking the worst of your opponent and remember that they have unlimited time and resources. Public-interest technologist, cybersecurity expert, and blogger, Bruce Schneier tells us:

> "History has taught us: never underestimate the amount of money, time, and effort someone will expend to thwart a security system. It's always better to assume the worst. Assume your adversaries are better than they are. Assume science and technology will soon be able to do things they cannot yet. Give yourself a margin for error. Give yourself more security than you need today. When the unexpected happens, you'll be glad you did."[21]

Give yourself more security than you need today. I really like that. In fact, indestructible security is the only thing that keeps any network or devices out of harm's way. But where do you start? Let's take a look at some of my top survival tips against being hacked. These include education and training, a well-executed HR policy, file access and file location, updates, backups, and much more.

We all know that employee negligence is a major cause of network breaches. The 2020 SolarWinds supply chain attack provides us with enough evidence of the fact. Research from Stanford University confirms that about 88% of all data breaches are caused by us humans.[22] More worryingly, 28% of these breaches impacted SMEs, businesses with fewer resources and financial clout than their corporate counterparts.[23] While hackers carry out planned attacks to exploit systems through phishing, password attacks, SQL injections, malware infection, and

DNS spoofing, underlying these crimes is usually an element of human error. A good portion of all security violations result from events such as delivering sensitive information to the wrong recipient or the insecure disposal of critical data.

How do we eradicate human error? A good place to start is cybersecurity education, which should underpin your staff onboarding processes and be followed through by regular ongoing training. All employees need to understand that they are part of what keeps business data secure. As such, they need to follow protocol and ensure that their devices are protected 24/7. If not, they become a weak link in an otherwise secure network. Cybersecurity education and training also encompasses having formal, written policies in place to keep data safe, which should be periodically reviewed. You can even go so far as to put your guys to the test. What could happen if you don't update this app? How do we make multiple backups? How often do I change my password? What are the alternatives to using MFA? When employees are correctly able to answer questions related to your cybersecurity, they are much more likely to follow protocol going forward.

Employees also need to realise that they will be held accountable if they violate IT policies and protocols. They should fully comprehend the nature of cyber threats and the severity of cyberattacks on any business. Make sure that everybody using a PC and accessing company data understands why good password practice and backup are vital to protect company data. Employees must be made aware that they should not use any devices without authorization and definitely not share their devices or passwords. Explain why unauthorized software and apps should never be installed on their work machines. Last, but by no means least, is email security. All staff should be able to identify spam and phishing emails, and you can even do some simulation testing to see if they do.

In Chapter 1, we spoke about spoofing emails, a type of cyberattack using emails with forged sender addresses. Often, recipients trust the alleged sender, open the email, and interact with its contents. That is where the trouble begins. Spoofing leads to phishing, which leads to ransomware. Train your employees to identify spoofing emails and websites. Does the displayed sender name match the email address? Is the information in the email signature accurate? Does the domain name have the correct extension? Are there any typos in the URL? Are the branding and fonts genuine or do they look suspect? Here you might need to make a close inspection and even look closely at the font used in a URL. For example, what is the difference between www.apple.com and www. аpple.com? In the second web address, the "а" is from the Cyrillic alphabet. Email security and ensuring that your DNS is set up correctly will also protect you against spoofing.

Unfortunately, cybersecurity education and training isn't the be-all and end-all. People are people, and they will always make mistakes, irrespective of how much training they receive or how frequently they receive it. Technology over people is what you need to protect your data.

In terms of HR procedure, you need to keep an up-to-date checklist of who can access what on your network. The same applies to your contractors and vendors. When an employee leaves, or you change vendors, ensure that access is revoked. According to research, 58% of companies have over 1,000 inactive user accounts.[24] SMEs don't fare well in this regard as they typically have even fewer processes around offboarding than corporates. I believe that it is vital to regularly review your relationships with staff, suppliers, and even customers. There should always be someone assigned to review relationships and delete unused or inactive accounts as required. A good analogy here is to liken your network to a surface area, and the number of accounts, those with access to the network, is proportional to the surface area. The more accounts you have, the greater the area. The greater the area, the greater the risk of entry by malicious actors. Put simply, when you minimize the surface area, you minimize the security risk. Remember that ghost user accounts, lying dormant and unnoticed, are easy targets for penetration by hackers.

Onboarding is equally as important as offboarding. Do you have an inventory of your network, its devices, and all the software used? And the same old question again - who has access to what? Is administrative access regulated? Do you have retention policies in place for emails, data, and logs? Is email archiving active? Is the data of a new starter, be it an employee or vendor, protected by storing it in a central location? That means you know where the data is and what the data is. Has the onboarded individual been thoroughly vetted? Have new suppliers and clients provided you with adequate documentation? These are questions that all need definitive answers.

HR, along with senior management, should also assign a key person who is responsible for your cybersecurity and data protection. Besides an important prerequisite for GDPR compliance, the cybersecurity officer needs to train, communicate, and increase security awareness across your entire SME and be held accountable. If a threat is identified or a breach occurs, they will need to isolate the vulnerability to prevent it from spreading through your whole network. Moreover, the person with assigned cybersecurity responsibility should be skilled in developing plans to prevent future incidents. They should also be able to recreate incidents in order to identify any vulnerabilities in your systems.

Another ticking time bomb is access overload. It's being said that 88% of companies with over 1 million folders have 10% of their folders open to everybody. An unlikely scenario for an SME, but this statistic isn't: 41% of companies have over 1,000 sensitive files open to everybody.[25] In other words, everyone can access an enormous amount of data without being monitored. So much for zero trust. How do we rectify the situation? You need to review who has access to what and only give access permissions to those who need it - this is the so-called "least privilege model." It's also important to be consistent with assigning permissions to folders - not one individual one day and another the next. When you simplify your access management procedures, it helps to lock down the potential exposure from insider threats.

File location, meaning where files are stored, and backups are another two top survival tips against hacking. I recommend that all of your folders and files be stored on a centralised system - a local server, cloud storage, or both. Again, as a reminder, if you are using a cloud server, it still needs management, password policies, security rules, updates, and, of course, backups. Just because you are using the cloud, don't assume that the cybersecurity basics are covered. There's a likelihood that they aren't. As I am writing this, I am aware that some of these issues are unheard of in larger organisations. Nevertheless, these are the real world, ground zero challenges that SMEs and microbusinesses face.

Files should not be stored locally on workstations and definitely not on mobile devices, which can easily get lost or stolen. I've said it before, and I'll say it again - backup is king! In Chapter 1, I mentioned the 3-2-1 rule for backups, where encrypted backups are stored on more than one medium isolated in different locations. But being a backup king goes beyond where and how you store your data. You need peace of mind knowing that you have high data retention. Many of us do not understand what data retention is and find the terminology confusing. It basically means how many versions or changes can you make to a folder or a file and restore at that point in time. In other words, if I made changes on a document 15 days ago, can I restore it to that point? As simple as that! On World Backup Day, technology executive and entrepreneur, Steven Santamaria echoed my sentiments:

> "The world's most valuable resource is data, and it is of utmost importance to properly store, protect, and preserve this resource. The safekeeping of data is essential because it represents the foundation upon which many modern businesses are built, and its loss can have far-reaching consequences for organizations and individuals alike. As such, ensuring the safety and longevity of data should be a top priority for any entity that relies on this precious resource."[26]

Firewalls and antivirus are insufficient to stave off a hacker. You need complete visibility of traffic both on and off your network, and continuous monitoring will achieve this. Continuous monitoring of traffic will nip any hacker or cyberattack in the bud. To maintain effective monitoring, make sure that all your systems are regularly and automatically updated with the latest security releases. If time and budget allow, you can go as far as doing regular data at risk discovery that will identify everything on your network and workstations that might be sensitive, from personal identifiable information (PII) to credit card details. This approach is the best way to protect your data from hackers.

The last of my top tips all revolve around passwords and logins. Forget 123456, QWERTY, or the name of your pet. You need indestructible passwords that are almost impossible to crack. Linked to this, you need to enforce a strict password policy, requiring passwords of a minimum length, a high level of complexity, and ones that have historically never been d. Also, if a device comes with a default password, log in and change it immediately to something complex and unguessable. The words of American actor Zachary Quinto provide a good rule of thumb for implementing a password policy:

> "I changed all my passwords. I have no two passwords that are the same for any service online. I have two-step verification enabled on all my devices... so yeah, I did take some extra steps that I hadn't taken before being exposed to this world."[27]

I strongly recommend using a password manager with a vault that stores encrypted credentials and shared passwords. You also need different levels of access within your SME. Help your team by creating an email notification before the password expiry date. That way, they'll expect to change their passwords before the actual event. Implementing single sign-on (SSO) is also highly recommended. SSO means that multiple applications can be accessed via a single user ID. It boosts security and makes disabling accounts much easier. With SSO, the password policies that you have implemented will also apply to all the connected systems. SSO is critical to help SMEs simplify security in general.

Two-step checks or MFA should not only be used for your network and online accounts. MFA should also apply to transactions such as bank transfers in which identity confirmation is given over the phone or via a text or WhatsApp message. If you need to share login credentials, never ever send them together. Sent the username via email and chose another communication medium for the password. This should only apply when if you are not using a password manager. However, at the very least, always use two mediums when you are sharing credentials. Never, ever send them on the same medium.

So, there you have it - my top survival tips to prevent you from being hacked. A long list? A big ask? Maybe, yes. But cybercrime prevention is well within reach, attainable, and affordable when you look in the right place. I know that effective cyber hygiene and cybersecurity practices only require applying some basic principles that are neither expensive nor complex. Think of KISS as a go-to reminder of how things can be for your cybersecurity - keep it simple and straightforward.

4

What About the Future?

> "To disrupt a country, halt major commercial flows or make important financial gains, hackers usually look for vulnerabilities that have not yet been discovered. The constant technological evolution is a catalyst for them to find new flaws to exploit."[1]

That's the take on hacking and future cybersecurity challenges based on predictions from the World Economic Forum. And as hackers look into the future, where do you think they'll start? My answer to that question is maybe an obvious one. They'll start with victims that are easy to prey on and paralyze - SMEs and microenterprises. Some of the future IT challenges that these small businesses are likely to encounter include migration to the cloud, lack of awareness, lack of standards, the value of education and training, and risk assessments.

More and more companies, SMEs to boot, are moving to the cloud and adopting cloud services such as Software-as-a-Service (SaaS). Cloud computing is often seen as a data solution that saves money and supports efficiency and scalability. It also facilitates remote working in our post-pandemic, work-from-home world. The global cloud computing market is predicted to be approximately $800 billion before the end of the decade.[2] Former U.S. Federal CIO Vivek Kundra spells out some of the benefits of using the cloud:

> "Just like water from the tap in your kitchen, cloud computing services can be turned on or off quickly as needed. Like at the water company, there is a team of dedicated professionals making sure the service provided is safe, secure, and available on a 24/7 basis. When the tap isn't on, not only are you saving water, but you aren't paying for resources you don't currently need."[3]

But here's the rub. Is the cloud really as safe and secure as Kundra makes out? I think not. SMEs migrating to the cloud are often not cloud-ready. Servers and applications are not configured properly, and this poses a major security risk. It is a known fact that incorrectly configured cloud solutions result in data breaches. The cloud also operates outside any network perimeter, so it is possible for the bad guys to access an SME's cloud-based services without authorization. Wily hackers could then remotely access sensitive data and even change or falsify data using stolen credentials.

Another challenge for SMEs using the cloud is potential data loss, aka data leaks. If the security of a cloud vendor is breached, attackers can gain access to critical data. This data is also subject to control by the cloud provider. If the provider is breached, what then? The SME loses its critical data and intellectual property and may be liable for regulatory non-compliance and breach of its customers' data. The International Data Corporation tells us that within 18 months of moving to the cloud, 79% of companies had at least one cloud data breach.[4]

When the media reports a cyberattack, think big. The papers want headliners with big numbers and potentially even bigger losses. Incidents that befall SMEs or micros seldom, if ever, make the press. These small businesses are lulled into a false sense of security, thinking, "It will never happen to us." The University of Salford Manchester captures this train of thought perfectly:

> "No one needs our data since we're such a small business, and we're not generating hundreds of millions of dollars in profit here."[5]

So, SMEs blissfully continue to think that cybersecurity is unimportant and continue to do nothing or the bare minimum. Unfortunately, it does happen to them and more often than they can imagine. SMEs are typically victims of ransomware and phishing, with employees considered to be the so-called weakest link. This situation was exacerbated by the pandemic, where remote and home working became the rule of thumb.

Implementing security solutions remotely and in isolation meant that 54% of SMEs in the UK experienced some form of cyberattack in 2022, an increase of 39% compared to 2020. As a ballpark, it cost them an average of £4,200 per incident.[6] Some SMEs operate on such a shoestring budget that they are unlikely to fully recover from the attack, financially or reputationally. I don't foresee this notion of ignorance and lack of awareness going away any time soon. Ultimately, those SMEs will do nothing until it is too late. Then they'll realize that cybersecurity isn't a zero-sum game.

SMEs thinking that they are in a cyber comfort zone is exacerbated by the fact that there are no enforceable cybersecurity standards as there are for data protection and privacy with the likes of GDPR. I find this surprising, considering SMEs are regarded as the most active enterprises in the global and UK economies. Obviously, a rigorous information security management standard like ISO 27001 would be too much for small operations - well beyond the scope of their security needs and budgets. But when you think that in the UK, there are 5.5 million SMEs, which make up 99.9% of private sector businesses[7], shouldn't there be some enforced basic cybersecurity standards? I'd like to think of this as much more than a safety net. Rather, it's the right way to do business. A Minimum Required Framework sets the precedence as a security standard, a safety net, and a safe and secure way to work for SMEs.

Now, I'll grant you that education does carry some weight in terms of providing awareness but months of training will not prevent a user from clicking on that forbidden link. Just once is all it takes. I might sound like a stuck record, but we can't continue blaming humans and human error. Let's get this right once and for all and make technology secure using secure technology. Relying on people to maintain security is like building a house of cards in a hurricane.

Now, let's talk about risk and risk assessment. Imagine that you've done a thorough security risk assessment and left no stone unturned. That means you know all the cybersecurity risks facing your SME, right? Wrong. Particularly off the mark if the assessment is a one-off. A decent security risk assessment is an ongoing evaluation of your risks and vulnerabilities and also an understanding of the threats they pose to your business. Let's read how Gartner defines cyber risk:

> "The potential for an unplanned, negative business outcome involving the failure or misuse of IT."[8]

There are two words from this definition that I'd like to highlight - *potential* and *unplanned.* Those are two elements that no risk assessment can iron out or negate. I'd say a good risk assessment is an accurate prediction of what could fail or be misused. It's not definitive.

Let's look at risk assessment in another way. Imagine your data is buried in the deepest bunker, far beneath the surface of the Earth. Only you have the key. You would assume that the bunker is at a very low risk of failure or being misused. It's not. Earthquakes happen. Fires happen. You could lose the key, or somebody could steal it. The long and the short is that risk assessments don't indicate how vulnerable networks and data really are. When you need to give someone access to files in your secure bunker, it will essentially be as secure as the device they use to access the data. The rule remains that the system is as secure as its weakest link. It doesn't matter how many millions you have or are spending on keeping the bunker secure.

So far, we've looked at the challenges SMEs face in the future based on what I've seen and know. They aren't cloud-ready. They lack awareness. There aren't any standards governing their cybersecurity. Education and training don't equate to cybersecurity solutions. Business owners are deluded into thinking that risk assessments provide an accurate picture of their cyber hygiene and cybersecurity.

The long and the short is that at the moment, we have a big problem. If we could control and ensure that SMEs had these cybersecurity basics in place, the majority of cyber risk would disappear - much like reducing the risk of an accident when your car has an MOT. We need to find a way to relegate and have complete and clear visibility on how systems are configured - these is the MOT for your business.

The challenge is that business owners dominate the rules and IT companies not willing to walk away. They are often enablers of misconfiguration and setups. IN dire cases, they let the owner or office manager DIY the company IT. The situation is exacerbated by buying into trends on the market and people lose focus on the big picture of their IT. Often there is a sudden obsession with a particular area of focus such as passwords, Dark Web scanning or incident response. People forget about the other bricks that make up the cybersecurity wall. You can't do that. To stay secure, you need all components as one doesn't work without the other.

But what about the unseen and unknown? How will AI and IoT, the cornerstones of emerging technologies, impact the cybersecurity of SMEs? The Organisation for Economic Co-operation and Development states that Artificial Intelligence (AI) is inherent to the digital transformation of SMEs.[9] Thinking about the Internet of Things (IoT), this affordable technology will give SMEs a competitive advantage, especially when aligned with automation and AI. The World Economic Forum claims that Industry 4.0 technologies like IoT will help SMEs attain sustainability.[10] All good news. But, as we all know, with anything new comes uncertainty. When translated into IT terms, this means greater cyber risk. In the next two chapters, we'll journey into the worlds of AI and IoT, exploring some of the main benefits for SMEs but looking closely at the cybersecurity risks that come with their adoption. You'll also meet two friends and colleagues of mine, respective experts in AI and IoT.

5

IoT in the Future– Get Smart and Stay Smart

> "If you think that the internet has changed your life, think again. The Internet of Things is about to change it all over again!"[1]
>
> – Brendan O'Brien

You would think those are the words of Bill Gates, Elon Musk, or another tech mogul. They're not. They come from the mouth of the now-deceased American voice actor Brendan O'Brien, made famous for his role as the original voice of Crash Bandicoot. While I'm not a fan of PS games, I am in full support of the Internet of Things (IoT) and Big Data. And IoT is big business. The global market was valued at about $661 billion in 2022 and is projected to be $3,352.97 billion by 2030.[2] That's a lot of money.

IoT has come a long way since John Romkey's 1989 toaster that could be turned on and off using a TCP/IP network. In 1992, there were only 1,000,000 IoT devices in the world. Now, there are more than 15 billion interconnected IoT devices talking to each other.[3] That number is expected to increase to 29 billion by 2030 and some say IoT devices could even surge to 125 billion.[4] That's somewhat of an exaggeration, I think. Nevertheless, the unprecedented surge in IoT devices, now more than double the human population, has been deemed an explosion of connected possibilities and vulnerabilities.[5]

IoT is much more than mobile phones, smart TVs, Alexa, and Siri. The IIoT, or Industrial Internet of Things, has been the main driving force for the fourth industrial revolution, Industry 4.0. This technology has penetrated industrial sectors in a big way, including retail, healthcare, IT and telecommunications, agriculture, and sustainable energy. At the moment, the manufacturing sector is the leading global investor in IoT. In Europe, the third-largest adopter of IoT behind North America and the Asia-Pacific region, the UK, Germany, and the Netherlands are considered to be leaders in IoT adoption, followed by the Nordics and countries in Eastern Europe.[6]

SMEs are also starting to buy into IoT technology. In 2021, 70% of UK small businesses were already looking into using IoT platforms to optimize operations, improve customer experience, and monitor their inventory.[7] Technologist, Christoph Burgdorfer, tells us that affordability is one of the reasons driving SMEs' adoption of IoT:

> "With hardware and software for IoT decreasing in price these kinds of applications are becoming increasingly commercially viable [for small and medium businesses]."[8]

I believe that there is much more to the proliferation of IoT than that it is easy on the wallet. IoT essentially means connectivity without human intervention. Industrial IoT is closely associated with other blossoming technologies such as 5G, Machine Learning (ML), big data, and AI. High bandwidths from 5G will mean that more devices can connect to the Internet. This means more data generation and processing capacity, which further increase the demand for ML and AI and allow companies of all sizes to benefit from big data. That said, the World Economic Forum tells us that SMEs face several challenges in IoT adoption, such as budgets to employ skilled workers, how to implement IoT effectively, and how to ensure an ROI.[9] Moving forward, these are all obstacles that can be overcome with good support and strategic planning.

So, if the world of IoT, with billions of devices and massive uptake generating enormous revenues, sounds too good to be true and that's probably because it is. Unfortunately, and particularly in the case of SMEs, there aren't many rules or standards in place to keep IoT security in check. On top of that, most people don't realize the risks that come with using IoT systems or how big of a challenge it is to keep them secure. With all these interconnected endpoints, it's a bit of a wild west out there for IoT security. Scott McLeod, a professor at the University of Colorado, claims that when it comes to IoT, individuals will opt for pleasure and convenience first and forget about the pain of being hacked that can easily follow:

> "There will be all kinds of hiccups, horror stories, accidents, deliberate acts of sabotage and other bumps along the road that will slow but not stop our greater connectivity. Convenience and empowerment always seem to win for most people, even at some loss of privacy, control or transparency."[10]

I completely agree. People are spellbound by the *magic* of connectivity and big data associated with IoT. IoT's rapid growth has meant that security has taken a backseat to speed and deployment. Typically, nonsecure protocols are usually used, and non-encrypted data is common. Living as we do in a plug-and-play generation, devices are frequently misplaced or misconfigured. And IoT manufacturers are also part to blame for the security vulnerabilities that abound. If a device doesn't work out of the box, it's unlikely to be a big seller.

With IoT, people forget security issues such as lack of visibility, limited security integration, poor testing, unpatched vulnerabilities, using weak passwords, or worse still, default passwords. In the worst cases, there are no passwords – by design you can password protect the device. This is not to mention the dangers of processing huge amounts of unsecured data from multiple endpoints. We need to remember that IoT devices and networks weren't really designed with security in mind, especially legacy ones. Ensuring the security of IoT devices can also be tricky because many smart devices have limited computing power and are susceptible to data leaks, malware infection, and other cyber risks. Security should be considered at the design phase of any IoT device. This will save time and effort later and avoid any potential embarrassment and financial loss in the future.

One sector deploying IoT that is particularly susceptible to hacking is the financial industry. Hackers, criminal syndicates, and gangs focus their efforts on financial institutions primarily due to the enticing profitability factor, where significant thefts can be accomplished with minimal effort. Extortion tactics often come into play, with the threat of relentless and disruptive distributed-denial-of-service (DDoS) attacks looming over their targets. In layman's terms, DDoS attacks involve sending an excessive amount of traffic to a website until it can no longer maintain the deluge of incoming requests. This means the website crashes and cannot provide the usual services as the overload of unnecessary requests mean that legitimate requests cannot be completed. Organizations either pay or face the threat of having their websites crushed by violent DDoS attacks. To fulfil their objectives, these cybercriminals frequently harness botnets, a network comprised of compromised private computers, devices, or IoT devices, all under their control without the owner knowing anything. The manipulation of these botnets is facilitated through specialized command and control (C&C) software and may encompass an array of devices, ranging from security cameras and DVD players to home routers. The UK Financial Conduct Authority (FCA) reported that 25% of all submitted cyber incidents in the first half of 2022 involved DDoS, compared to 4% in 2021.[11] In January 2017, the Lloyds Banking Group, consisting of Lloyds, Halifax and Bank of Scotland, suffered a massive 48-hour DDoS attack, with cybercriminals bombarding websites with millions of fake requests designed to grind the group's systems to a halt. Fortunately, no accounts were hacked or compromised in the attack, and Lloyds decided not to pay the ransom.[12]

Interview with Raj Rajarajan

But let's turn our attention to what's happening in the world of IoT at the moment and hear from an expert in the field. I had an interesting conversation with Zhero's own Head of Research and Development, Raj Rajarajan, about all things IoT and cybersecurity for SMEs. Raj is also a Professor of Security Engineering and the Director of the Multidisciplinary Centre of Cybersecurity for Society at City, University of London. Here's what he had to say about IoT and cybersecurity on a budget.

Izak: Hi Raj. Starting off with a general question. Why has IoT grown so rapidly in the last five to ten years?

Raj: I think the growth of IoT is due to the decentralized management of devices. This means that we are slowly moving away from a centralized single point of failure to a decentralized setting where we have multiple interconnected devices delivering a service. I think with COVID, which kicked in at the time, there was an inflation of IoT in the marketplace. People started moving across enterprise IoT devices into the domestic setting and also domestic IoT into the enterprise setting. There was no baseline security that you could define for the IoT setting. They are mostly in different segments in an organization, so it was very difficult to establish the cybersecurity of these interconnected devices that were disconnected from the core corporate network. This was then used as a hotspot by cybercriminals to launch cyberattacks through things like smart printers, smart cameras, and smart coffee machines that didn't have any built-in security from the start. That is the fundamental fault that caused more cyberattacks within the IoT enterprise network.

Izak: Just to take one step back, you're saying that because of COVID-19, IoT started to become much more popular in terms of corporate or business use? Traditionally, IoT was focused on use in homes and as sensors in industry.

Raj: Enterprise IoT wasn't as we now see [it] post-COVID. Organizations were not willing to let these devices within the enterprise network because they understood the inherent vulnerability that comes with them. With default passwords being used, people didn't want to use these devices with the secure enterprise.

Izak: What are the current threats and challenges facing enterprise IoT?

Raj: I think it goes back to the basics of adding usernames and passwords and configuring these devices correctly. Most of these devices are plug-

and-play, which means that you don't have a lot of control over the way that you can customize them. I still think the fundamental issue with IoT devices is using default passwords. Nobody seems to be taking this seriously, and most of the decent attacks have involved using user passwords, which are factory settings. These default settings are very easy to figure out.

Izak: So, you're saying, and sorry I'm acting dumb here, that IoT endpoints are much more vulnerable than other endpoints in a network?

Raj: Yes. Because they are decentralised, it is very difficult to see where they are connected to the rest of the network. They are in silos, network fragmentations that make it very complicated for a network operation or security operations centre to monitor these devices remotely. The perimeters are also not clearly defined, so you may be able to get access to the devices from outside the corporate network. This is why zero trust security has become very popular because it protects devices by following the guidelines that there is no trust. You need to continue to authenticate devices so that they are always monitored and authenticated. You don't authenticate once and then let them use it forever - that's dangerous.

Izak: You've kind of touched on my next question. What are the solutions to these challenges or threats, especially with IoT devices having default passwords and very little control? How will enterprise manage these?

Raj: I think the best way is not to integrate these devices into the corporate main infrastructure. You need to define boundaries, and if you really want to integrate them into the core network, then you need to have things like zero trust for continuous authentication to authenticate these devices. This should be based around physical parameters, logical parameters, and soft and hard biometrics. You continuously track and trace these devices and maintain their authenticity over a period of time. You do a spatial-temporal monitoring of these devices so that you are continuously making sure they're following the security policies of any organisation and they are not just logged in once, and then people can access the network forever.

Izak: Thanks, Raj. Okay, now on to SMEs. To what extent have they adopted, or need to adopt, IoT devices?

Raj: I think this is an interesting question. A lot of SMEs started using enterprise devices like enterprise Alexa, enterprise-based smart cameras, printers, and other devices mainly because they were easy to plug and play and could scale production quite quickly. At the same time, they haven't thought about how to look at the security of these devices. SMEs are quite vulnerable due to the way they are using IoT devices, and they don't understand the real threats that they pose. They need to spend some time and energy in developing a clear security policy… in terms of bringing your own devices. This is very important for SMEs that have several vendors, suppliers, and external entities that they work or collaborate with. They might not have devices with APIs that are security scanned, and you might allow them to use these devices within your network, and that could open it up to new types of attacks. SMEs really need to take this seriously in identifying the assets. I have spoken to SMEs and many don't even know the assets they own within their company. They haven't thought about IoT and focus on protecting laptops and desktops and mobiles. I think for SMEs, it's still a way to go before they start protecting IoT properly.

Izak: Are there any budgetary or financial constraints for SMEs regarding IoT?

Raj: IoT security is a new territory. There are cloud-based solutions for zero trust, but these are expensive packages. For most SMEs who focus on new and existing assets, this would be too expensive. Also, SMEs don't consider supply chain risks. Many small businesses are dependent on their suppliers, partners, and vendors.

Izak: In terms of addressing specific SME challenges, what solutions do you see or recommend?

Raj: I think, for smaller businesses, they need to make sure their devices have a password policy in place and definitely change the default password and other factory settings. The new passwords should follow the security policy of the organization. On top of this, they probably need to think about monitoring IoT using brokers - they can then see some of the threats they may be up against. They could also apply some kind of lightweight machine learning algorithms to basic traffic analysis to see if there are any spikes in the IoT network traffic. There are many products out there on the market for IoT monitoring. One challenge is what level of IoT penetration you have in the organization. The higher the number of devices, the more complex the monitoring becomes. Unlike a fixed network, in an IoT network, you have multiple devices that don't follow specific standards like PCs. This makes it a bit more complex because there is no solution that fits all. You need to do more customization and configuration based on these different devices. As you scale the implementation, you need to think about how to manage these devices. Automating the management of these devices could be the way forward, but they would need a lot of investment for SMEs.

Izak: Raj, with that in mind, something I've just thought of is about user access. Obviously, with a laptop or tablet, there is one user who has access. Do IoT devices not have multiple users, providing more of a threat at the endpoints?

Raj: Again, an interesting question. For example, there is an enterprise Alexa for scheduling calendars to which multiple people often have access. But Alexa does provide multi-layer security where the CEO of a company will have their own credentials and have greater access compared to, say, an executive secretary who has limited access to what they can do. Enterprise IoT allows you to define different layers of security.

Izak: Thanks, Raj. Last question for now. What role do you think IoT will play in business ten years from now? Or even beyond?

Raj: I think IoT will be used mainly for automating many of the existing functionalities within the industry sectors. Sectors like manufacturing, retail, finance, and others all use IoT to collect data. This is used to do more predictive intelligence in terms of the business or to improve performance and efficiency. For example, you can get quick to market when delivering certain products and services. If you can do real-time analysis of data, you may be able to provide better and more accurate services and achieve more efficiency. I think there are a lot of added benefits for productivity by using IoT in the future. IoT can also provide new business models. IoT has already shown a lot of potential in big supermarkets in countries like Singapore. They use sensors to track shopping behaviours in shopping malls and then use the data to identify clusters of people around types of food or clothing. This shows that some food or clothes are more popular than others. These insights are very useful in the design and development of new products. Remember that IoT is very sector-specific. The way the manufacturing sector uses IoT is very different from how banks use it. Think about commuting. In national train stations, there are now boards telling you which platforms are busy and which coaches are busy. This information can be used to avoid overcrowding in stations and on trains. In large organizations, they use IoT to monitor how occupied the offices are, and this helps to maintain the energy efficiency of the building. Again, I think we need to be very sector-specific in terms of the future of IoT.

Izak: Raj, thanks so much for your time. Is there anything you would like to add before we wind up?

Raj: I think the important thing is to emphasize the difference between IoT for enterprise and IoT for the industrial setting. In industry, IoT devices are used to control the programmable logic controllers in water management or energy smart grid distribution systems, for example. When we differentiate between enterprise and industrial IoT, we can then define the security controls for each. The future will definitely be around how to continuously monitor these devices and continuously authenticate these devices in a zero-trust environment. We need to use hardware and software security and not just username and password. We should also look at the typical behaviour of IoT devices. You can then see if there are any anomalies in behaviour. I really believe that authentication and zero trust are the future of IoT security.

Besides bringing his expertise in cybersecurity and IoT to the table, Raj also reiterates what I've said about going back to security basics. Things like not using default passwords, sticking to the company password policy, MFA, around-the-clock monitoring and reporting, having an inventory of assets, and everything else that applies to good cybersecurity and cyber hygiene. What applies to assets like workstations and Access points inside the network perimeter also applies to those on the edge, like IoT devices.

Adding to Raj's words of wisdom, I'd like to dedicate the rest of this chapter to further exploring some critical IoT security challenges. These are device management, password security, updates and patches, and the alarming skills gap we face in the IoT employment market. Why so much emphasis on IoT security? Because the challenges abound. Just to give you an idea, in the first half of 2021 alone, there were a staggering 1.51 billion breaches of IoT devices.[13] Clearly, IoT is a technology that needs thorough security controls in place. As Stephane Nappo, the Global Head of Information Security for Société Générale International Banking, tells us:

> "The Internet of Things devoid of comprehensive security management is tantamount to the Internet of Threats."[14]

I want to reinforce what Raj considers to be the biggest IoT threat and that is using default passwords. Any hard-coded or embedded credentials pose a threat to IT systems and are equally dangerous to IoT devices. Most of these come with a universal default password (UDP) such as *user*, *admin*, or *123456*. Guessable or hard-coded credentials provide an opportunity for hackers to attack the device directly. With default passwords, the attacker may already know the machine's password if they purchase the same device.

Let's look at the 2016 Mirai botnet attack as an example. Please note that I'm telling a watered-down version of the story to keep things simple. That year, attackers launched a massive DDoS attack on the website of a security company, Kerbs on Security, that was hosted on OVH, one of the largest web hosting providers in the world. The attack targeted DNS provider, DYN. DNS serves as the Internet's equivalent of a phonebook or global address book, facilitating the connection between web browsers and websites. Its primary function involves translating easily understandable domain names, such as www.amazon.com into machine-readable IP addresses like 192.0.2.44. On the first day of the attack in September, Mirai had infected 65,000 IoT devices. By November, this had soared to 600,000.[15] The infection of DYN prevented users from accessing popular online sites including Airbnb, Amazon, GitHub, HBO, Netflix, PayPal, Reddit, and Twitter. So how did these DDoS attacks happen, which some believe to be the largest of its kind in history? Mirai botnets infected IoT devices, such as routers and cameras that were operating on default passwords. Once infected, the hackers could use the devices to execute DDoS on a massive scale because there were so many of them.

How could we have avoided the Mirai disaster? Easy. Go back to the basics of good password practice. Default passwords should be changed immediately. If you buy a smart fridge with the username fridge and password 123456, change them without a thought. Remember, just like any other internet-connected technology, each IoT device needs a unique username and password. Attackers commonly also use brute-force attacks, in short, trying to guess commonly used credentials through millions and millions of login attempts. You can prevent these by having account lockouts after a few failed login attempts, using CAPTCHA, and using MFA. What about universal plug-and-play (UPnP)? UPnP is a protocol that lets networked devices automatically open a port on the router to facilitate communication with your IoT device remotely. If you don't need remote access, then disable UPnP. And, as Raj told us, use zero trust for authentication. Authenticating just once isn't enough.

I next want to touch on the importance of firmware updates. By design, IoT products are created with usability and connectivity in mind. The good news is that they may be secure at the time of purchase. However, as time goes by, they become vulnerable as hackers discover new security flaws or bugs. This needs to be fixed with regular updates. So, don't be lazy. When updates are available, apply them. If you don't, your will devices become more and more vulnerable. Also ensure that the software you use, like the apps on your phone, is updated when using your IoT device.

Following on from the Mirai attacks, a new variant of the botnet, known as Satori, was discovered in late 2017. The malware used hard-coded exploits to target IoT devices, attacking as many as 700,000 in total.[16] Satori typically preyed on poorly secured IoT devices, including home digital video recorders (DVRs), surveillance cameras, and enterprise networking equipment. Besides having weak passwords, they also had firmware vulnerabilities. Put simply, they became proponents of DDoS attacks because they hadn't been updated.

All these IoT nightmare stories may sound foreign and far away from us. In reality, they happen. We recently provided consultancy to a solar farm that had been hacked using some of the measuring instruments and devices that provided critical operating information. To our shock and horror, default passwords were used, their network was completely exposed and there was not access control from the outside. Our risk assessment concluded that there was absolutely no regulation controlling who or what could access data and from what. So, to reiterate, these are real-life issues.

What about device management? Many IoT and IoMT (Internet of Medical Things) are unmanaged and are running unsupported legacy operating systems and software. Companies, from corporates to SMEs, also don't know how many active devices they have or what they are. Unmanaged devices are a prime ransomware target, especially in healthcare. So, what are the basic solutions here? Update the OS and software if you can. If not, it's time to invest in new gear. Also, as I've said before, keep an updated inventory of all your assets. I mean, what's the use of having it if you don't know that you've got it?

There's also a significant lack of skills and upskilling in the field of IoT. This remains a barrier to the deployment of the technology, especially in SMEs that are reliant on in-house IT support. Business leader, Mike Crater tells us:

> "The IoT skills gap is a major concern for today's enterprises. For IoT to be a sustained success, access to the relevant skill sets is needed at all levels. Without all these skill sets in place, businesses will continue to struggle to make the best use of the data they gather, to integrate IoT projects into the wider organization and benefit from the transformative role that IoT can play in the global supply chain."[17]

My take on it is that if you are using IoT and don't have people skilled in it, you are letting trouble through the front door. To close the IoT skills gap, SMEs need to upskill or hire part-time or contract employees with the appropriate expertise. Also, consider the type of people you are recruiting. Do they see the big picture, just as you do? Are they willing to embrace a changing technological landscape that includes IoT? If you want to do IoT on more of a shoestring, you can always outsource to address the skills gap. This may save you time and money, but you'll be much less in control of which IoT devices access your network and by whom.

There are three security pillars of IoT - confidentiality, integrity, and availability. Confidentiality means you know your data is protected from unauthorised access. When working with sensitive data on your IoT device, you need to create a dedicated network, as IoT devices are by design always vulnerable. Using a virtual local area network or VLAN will place them in isolation and will always be your first line of defence. Integrity is the fact that you can trust your data. Availability is, I think quite clear - your data must always be available. With these three pillars in mind, reflect on the advice Mr. Weasley gives Harry in *Harry Potter and the Chamber of Secrets*:

> "Never trust anything that can think for itself if you can't see where it keeps its brain."[18]

Even without the three pillars or not, this statement applies now more than ever to this global outpouring of the Internet of Things. Unfortunately, the vulnerability issues associated with IoT are unlikely to disappear anytime soon because of the competitive nature of the IoT industry and the costs involved to improve security. But there are things you can do to protect yourself. Besides isolating your network, you can do regular backups, update and patch regularly, limited access, use encryption, monitor all the devices on your network, and train your employees. Sadly, we all in the habit of 'set and forget' but essentially that is dropping the ball on security. While embracing and enjoying the benefits of technology is the way forward, dropping the ball and compromising security is something we should never do.

Professor Muttukrishnan Rajarajan - Director, Centre for Cybersecurity at City, University of London and Head of Research and Development, Zhero Limited

Professor Muttukrishnan Rajarajan or Raj, is one of the top achievers in cybersecurity in the UK. As Zhero's Head of Research & Development, Raj's primary IT focus is research, but he also believes in cybersecurity in action and emphasises the product as much as the process. As a pioneer of cybersecurity research, Raj has been the Professor of Security Engineering at City, University of London since 2012 as well as the Director of the Institute for Cybersecurity. Since February 20122, he has part of the UK Cabinet Office's initiative on Digital Government, focusing on Identity Assurance. The Prof's wide-ranging knowledge and experience include privacy-preserving data management, IoT privacy, network intrusion detection, cloud security, and identity management

6

The Impact of AI and Automation—Bittersweet Transformation

> "Mark my words, AI is far more dangerous than nukes…why do we have no regulatory oversight? I am not normally an advocate of regulation and oversight… I think one should generally err on the side of minimizing those things…but this is a case where you have a very serious danger to the public."[1]
>
> – Elon Musk

Those were the words Elon Musk uttered at a tech conference in Texas in 2018, long before the arrival of ChatGPT and other generative AI creatures. I often blow hot and cold with Elon and his words, but nowhere near on the same level as my love-hate relationship with ransomware. In this instance, I think Musk makes a very good point. The human-AI relationship does have the potential to be a bittersweet one. Sure, businesses, including SMEs, can benefit tremendously from AI automation, but the technology does come with inherent threats, especially in the world of IT and cybersecurity. But I'm running ahead of myself here. Before looking at what we can do to minimize any of the risks that AI poses, let's see why it has become so popular. To put the scale of AI in perspective, reflect on what Bill Gates says:

> "If you invent a breakthrough in artificial intelligence, so machines can learn, that is worth 10 Microsofts."[2]

And if Gates thinks AI could be worth 10 Microsofts, then it's obviously worth its weight in gold. The fact that the UK AI market is valued at £17 billion by the US International Trade Administration clearly supports Gates's claim. By 2035, this is expected to be £800 billion.[3] Also, based on research by the UK government, one in six UK organisations, totalling 432,000, have embraced at least one AI technology. The breakdown here is 68% of large companies, 33% of medium-sized companies, and 15% of small companies, with SMEs making up 48% of the total.[4]

AI has come a long way since Alan Turing released his paper titled *Computing Machinery and Intelligence* in 1950. Virtual assistants (VAs) were born in 2011 when Apple released Siri, the first voice-activated VA with natural language interaction for smartphones. Following Apple's lead, Google released Google Now in 2012, Microsoft introduced Cortana in 2014, and Amazon launched Echo/Alexa in the same year. However, besides robotics, I think the real breakthrough for businesses was when OpenAI launched ChatGPT, the chatbot based on GPT-3, or Generative Pre-trained Transformer 3, a machine learning language prediction model. ChatGPT operates with 175 billion parameters, 570GB of text data, and 300 billion words. That's almost an incomprehensible amount of data.[5]

ChatGPT and other generative language models are setting the trend in AI technology at the moment. What sets ChatGPT apart from other chatbots is its ability to communicate in a manner that closely resembles human language. It has been fine-tuned for a wide range of language generation tasks, including question-answering, language translation, and long and short-form writing. This creates a unique opportunity for all businesses, including SMEs, to explore new ways of streamlining their operations. From automation to communication and research, you can leverage ChatGPT and other AI technologies to address different pain points for internal use and to enhance the customer experience.

A big plus is that automation relies on AI rather than human labour. Just think about online banking and chatbots for online shopping, for example. Businesses can automate departments such as accounting, social media and marketing, sales, software development, customer support, and HR. ChatGPT's analytical capabilities also extend beyond ideation, enabling it to perform complex processes such as supply chain management and financial planning using real-time data. ChatGPT can help streamline your operations with data entry and appointment scheduling, reducing the risk of errors, improving data accuracy, and increasing efficiency and effectiveness. When you use ChatGPT to reduce manual labour, your team has much more time to focus on creative and uniquely human tasks. Using AI for automation will save you money, boost productivity, and surely strengthen your bottom line. The Organisation for Economic Co-operation and Development (OCED) states that AI is vital to the digital transformation of SMEs.[6]

> "AI can affect and benefit SMEs in two ways: by altering their business environment and easing the conditions under which they do business, or by enabling them to change their business models and practices, which could ultimately allow them to increase productivity and outreach, and scale-up."

The OCED also states that AI has seen rapid uptake in the sectors of transport, finance, marketing and advertising, science, healthcare, security, and the public sector. And with the global artificial intelligence market size valued at $136.55 billion, it all sounds too good to be true.[7] It is. Nothing can be that good without some bad.

Let's start with one of my favourites (not) - malware. ChatGPT has already been used for malicious purposes by bad actors with limited-to-zero cyber skills. This obviously raises the alarm that the chatbot could democratize the creation of evasive malware or more sophisticated social engineering and phishing emails. Regarding the use of chatbots to create spear phishing malware for targeted or customised attacks, cyber researchers Eran Shimony and Omer Tsarfati tell us:

> "The malware created using ChatGPT could easily evade security products and make mitigation cumbersome with very little effort or investment by the adversary."[8]

The impact of democratized cybercrime has been seen with the rise of RaaS on the online ransomware marketplace. All I can say is that it is critical for organisations to take steps to protect themselves from this possibility. ChatGPT has even recommended these precautions:

> "To minimize the risk of ChatGPT-generated malware, it is essential to follow sound security practices, such as access controls, monitoring, and secure data storage."[9]

Highly evasive adaptive threat (HEAT) attacks are a relatively new and rapidly expanding type of attack vector that is capable of penetrating multiple layers of security software, including firewalls, secure web gateways, and phishing detection. Some researchers asked ChatGPT if it was capable of carrying out HEAT attacks. Unfortunately, the adage "if you can't take the HEAT, get out of the kitchen" doesn't apply to AI. To the query, ChatGPT responded:

> "It is possible for ChatGPT or any other language model to be misused to generate malware. If a malicious actor has access to the model and trains it on malware samples, it could generate malicious code or be used to create phishing campaigns or other nefarious activities. In this sense, ChatGPT generated malware could be considered a HEAT threat, as AI-generated malware can be sophisticated, adaptive, and difficult to detect."[10]

To that end, the chatbot is unable to create malware without input. However, it is more than capable of being an accomplice to phishing scams and ransomware attacks.

To protect themselves against HEAT attacks, I recommend that SMEs incorporate isolation technology into their cybersecurity strategies. This ensures that all active content is executed in a cloud-based, isolated browser rather than on the user's device. It shifts the focus away from post-compromise detection and towards prevention, working to ensure that malicious payloads never reach the targeted endpoint. With HEAT attacks becoming increasingly more popular and the potential for future implications arising from the abuse of intelligent systems such as ChatGPT, SMEs must update their defenses to guard against these sophisticated modern attack methods. As I've said before, stick to the basics of cyber security, and everything else should take care of itself. You don't need to throw the baby out with the bathwater.

I'm far from being a gloom monger but remember that phishing attacks are often where we are most susceptible and also the root cause of most ransomware infections. Hackers using generative AI may be able to translate their phishing attacks into multiple languages better, and chatbot-style applications can automate parts of the back-and-forth messages with potential victims. They can also mimic tone and style, making it more difficult for the end user to differentiate between a genuine or phishing email. This is particularly problematic for business email compromise (BEC), a type of attack where hackers try to trick C-suite executives into revealing sensitive and confidential information, or into transferring funds. This doesn't mean SMEs are destined to succumb to AI-generated malware. Not at all. It just means being on high alert and always being aware of your security practices. The same basics will always apply, even to artificial intelligence. As we know, these are good password management, updating regularly, backing up, MFA, monitoring and reporting, and everything else we've looked at.

On a positive note, AI and machine learning can enhance and improve email security. This happens by faster and more accurate threat detection. Automated approaches to email security could alleviate administrative burdens on their already stretched security teams. At the moment, most SMEs don't use AI or machine learning for email security and to prevent BEC. However, I predict that this will rapidly change in the near future as the dark side of AI becomes more of a threat.

I'd like to take AI security awareness one step further. When you add any new app to your IT network, it potentially creates new vulnerabilities that could be exploited to gain access to other areas in your network. Generative AI like ChatGPT or Google's Bard pose a unique risk because they contain complex algorithms that make it difficult for developers to identify security flaws. We also know that AI applications are developing and spreading like wildfire. The normal controls on software development and lifecycle management may not always be present. I think is quite easy for a skilled and ill-intending developer to disguise an AI app as a genuine product or service. Fake AI software and apps obviously have privacy, security, and anonymity concerns. My advice is not to download or install anything that looks suspicious. Remember that fake apps can mimic the look and feel of genuine ones. Icons may be the same, the dashboard may appear familiar, and they may even be available from trusted sources like Google Play, Microsoft Store, Apple Store, or Apple Business Manager. Always check the app with the name of the developer. Check the number of downloads. If the app is popular and useful, this will be a big number. You could also check the reviews, although the bad guys out there also post fake reviews about their fake products. I would also check permissions. If an app is asking for something it doesn't need, then that's a big red flag. For example, if a video streaming app randomly wants permission to access your smartphone or workstation's camera and microphone, that's a no-no. Last but not least, I advise scanning with a reliable anti-malware app before installing anything.

My associate and friend, Ben Azvine, believes that AI will play a critical role in IT network security. He says:

> "We are taking AI and making it help humans to be better… We are more about the Iron Man version of AI than the Terminator version."[11]

Ben believes that as the number of connected devices continues to surge, traditional methods of safeguarding assets have become obsolete. Today, organisations, including network operators, must adopt a cybersecurity approach that encompasses three essential phases: prevention, detection/prediction, and response. The response phase must be significantly expedited compared to previous practices, aiming for hours rather than days. Meanwhile, achieving effective detection/prediction necessitates the utilisation of advanced analytics and AI algorithms.

It's also important to realise that we share more via AI than we think and this includes IoT-driven AI such as Siri and Alexa. There is an enormous amount of data collected, used, and dumped, which results in an elevated risk of data breaches and identity theft. Of course, it's unlikely that Apple or Amazon would do anything with your data as their reputation is at stake. But watch out for what and who you share data with, especially customers' sensitive information. With that terrific computational power comes the risk of data leaks. Confidential corporate or proprietary data is often processed by AI, meaning that data leaks could expose sensitive information, including sensitive client data and strategic data. Just for a chuckle and a break from the serious side of things, check out this dialogue between Siri and a user. It also makes me question the reliability of artificial intelligence.

Siri: What can I help you with?

User: Siri, I'm bleeding really bad. Can you call me an ambulance?

Siri: From now on, I'll call you "An Ambulance," OK?

AI and data sharing go hand in hand. Responsible data sharing using AI means SMEs can implement and sustain a customer-centric, integrated business model that provides greater efficiency, flexibility, and increased visibility. But the emphasis is on the word *responsible*. Your data sharing will need to be compliant with regulations such as the GDPR. Again, you will have to implement access control and apply a zero-trust model. To repeat myself, only give access to those who need it and when they need it. Also, be aware that AI can extract data from data, including implicit sensitive information. This means that data privacy becomes even more important. If something is online, it's never 100% secure. When data is shared using AI, it's processed and stored in the cloud, so there is always the risk of a data breach. So, limit the information you share, be cautious with highly sensitive data, review your app's privacy policies, and, if possible, anonymize your data.

Another aspect of AI that I'd like to touch on is deep fakes. And I'm not talking about students using ChatGPT to cheat on their coursework or illicit images of Tom Cruise or Donald Trump. Voice and facial recognition are being used more as an access control security measure. AI is an opportunity for bad actors to create deepfakes that get around that security. To me, that spells danger - identity theft of the worst kind. The good news is that big tech firms like Google, Microsoft, and Meta have taken a strong stand against deepfake technology. They're actively involved in developing tools to detect and combat its misuse. Microsoft is at the forefront of creating innovative anti-deepfake technology, exemplified by their project, the Microsoft Video Authenticator.

Google, the owner of YouTube, has made it crystal clear that it's committed to preventing the spread of deep fake content.

Unfortunately, good intentions aren't always good enough. We have yet to reach a point where we can reliably discern genuine content from fabricated ones. While there are several notable tools available, such as Counter.social, DeepTrace, Reality Defender, and Sensity.ai, which touts itself as the world's inaugural deep fake detection tool, the most effective deep fake detectors currently attain only a 65% accuracy rate. It's worth noting that even Azure Cognitive Services, a prominent player in the field, struggled, being deceived over 78% of the time.[12] The words of James Bores, an experienced cybersecurity consultant, don't bring any joy to the party either:

> "In terms of what people can do, the depressing answer is not much. There are tools to try and detect AI-generated content, but they are unreliable. Some of them work, and some of them don't, and these will only become more unreliable as the technology gets better."

The best you can do is to be aware and be vigilant. Also, you can take on a social responsibility role by reporting anything suspicious to a tech giant or social media platform. The more we watch over each other, the less there is for us to watch out for.

At the end of the day, I'm by no means advocating that SMEs should avoid automation and AI. The benefits definitely outweigh the risks, provided you apply thorough digital risk management to your data and network, leaving no stone unturned. SMEs also don't have to bear the financial outlay of developing their own costly and complex AI systems. There are many, including cloud-based vendors of Software-as-a-Service (SaaS) and Machine-Learning-as-a-Service (MLaaS), including Google, Microsoft, Amazon, and IBM. SaaS delivers pre-configured data structures and pre-trained AI models for SMEs to leverage, including solutions like cloud-based enterprise resource planning (ERP) and customer relationship management (CRM). On the other hand, MLaaS platforms offer automated or partially automated machine learning services that utilize diverse data sources, enabling more extensive customisation compared to SaaS. For example, we embrace AI and consistently develop bespoke apps to facilitate the automation of processes, combining security with simplicity and affordability. That said, everything we build is with security in mind. Thankfully, nowadays many of the email security providers are adopting AI to help them with more advanced intelligence and security. I honestly believe that AI is an enabler of SMEs, allowing them to leapfrog to the next level, scale, and become more competitive. Remember that we need to find a balance between what is practical and increases productivity, and at the same time always be in control.

I'd like to dedicate the last part of this chapter by sharing with you a chat about AI and cybersecurity for SMEs that I had with an associate of mine, Pranava Madhyastha. Pranava is a Senior Lecturer in Computer Science at City, University of London and an expert in AI and Machine Learning.

Interview with Pranava Madhyastha

Izak: Hi, Pranava. Let's start with a more general question about AI in business. What accounts for the rapid growth of AI and investment in AI in the last five years?

Pranava: I think businesses have seen the benefits of using automation to accelerate growth. AI saves a lot of time and money doing many routine tasks that, otherwise, people would need to do. So, investing money in AI means that many daily tasks are automated and that people can put their skills to better use. AI has also grown rapidly because it has moved away from code to become much more of a language model like ChatGPT. Large language models are much easier to use as people can use almost any language as an input instead of being skilled in coding. These large language models also have a rapid response time and deliver accurate outputs. I believe this has also been a major factor influencing the take up of AI by businesses.

Izak: To what extent has this growth been driven by business needs or technological advancements? Or both?

Pranava: I think it's a bit of both. Businesses, including SMEs, have seen how automation and AI can make them more effective and productive and accelerate their growth. As the needs of business have increased, so has the need or demand for automation, and this has been a driving factor in developing AI technology.

Izak: What are the current cybersecurity threats and challenges with using AI?

Pranava: One of the main challenges of using generative AI like ChatGPT, for example, is the ability for the model to create content that looks like it has come from a real person when it actually hasn't. So here I speak of cybersecurity threats like business email compromise and, of course, phishing and other scams. Generative AI can also be used for deepfake social engineering attacks, which can easily deceive users. I also think another threat is the huge volume of data handled by AI platforms offered by companies like Amazon, Google, and Microsoft. These all transmit data using APIs, and when the data is highly sensitive or personal, this could become a security issue. Also, as AI tools become cheaper and, in some cases, free of charge, the risks of this technology to cybersecurity will be even greater.

Izak: What are the solutions to these threats and challenges?

Pranava: Unfortunately, emails and other content like deep fakes produced by AI can be very convincing as these models use huge amounts of data as a generative resource. I think the usual cybersecurity precautions need to be taken, like not clicking on a suspicious-looking link or not downloading a suspicious-looking attachment. Also, training and awareness are very important. Employees need to be aware that emails, images, and other content can easily come from non-trusted sources, even if they look legitimate. When it comes to data protection, businesses need to add as many layers of protection and security as possible to make sure that data isn't hacked or leaked. I also recommend having detection mechanisms in place to mitigate any potential cyber threats.

Izak: To what extent have SMEs adopted AI and machine learning?

Pranava: I think this depends on the extent of automation they need or have adopted. There are some relatively cheap AI models out there for automation that won't put SMEs out of pocket. As such, many UK SMEs have embraced AI technology to automate day-to-day tasks. Also, many SMEs are using generative AI as a starting point or scaffold, which they can then build on. This will only increase despite the lack of a regulatory framework.

Izak: What are the benefits of SMEs adopting AI?

Pranava: This goes back to what I said earlier about accelerating growth. SMEs usually have small teams where workers can be stretched. When routine tasks can be automated, then the team can focus on streamlining the business and accelerating growth. Another benefit is that automating tasks with AI gets rid of human error - or most of it. Automating with AI will help SMEs become more competitive. Many SMEs find driving new sales, cutting costs, and recruiting the best talent challenging. We've seen that AI helps to boost sales, improve marketing, and improve customer support.

Izak: What are the specific threats and challenges for SMEs using AI?

Pranava: The obvious ones are what we've already discussed - becoming victims of phishing scams and business email compromise. One challenge that SMEs adopting AI face is a limited budget. Off-the-shelf AI is usually affordable, but it becomes expensive if the model has to be tailored for specific jobs or functions. This can become even more expensive if they need to hire an expert programmer to develop and run the AI software.

Izak: What are the solutions to these specific threats and challenges?

Pranava: From a cyber perspective, I see training and awareness as one solution. In terms of creating bespoke software, I think the SME should really weigh up the benefits of automation. If the investment is really worth it, then it might be worth considering. Otherwise, I would recommend using existing AI software and large language models.

Izak: Which sectors have seen the greatest uptake in AI and why?

Pranava: I don't think you can single out one or [even] just a few sectors. All sectors can and do benefit from AI. But there are a few sectors I'd like to highlight. In healthcare, for example, using AI means more accurate record-keeping, potentially more accurate diagnosis and appropriate treatment plans, and also providing 24/7 services and support. AI in the medical profession also reduces human error. In the postal service, AI can be used for scanning parcels for customs duty. This would otherwise be a time-consuming and tedious manual task. AI models can be trained to recognize patterns such as shape, size, and weight and then generate outputs using machine learning. In the hospitality sector, AI has many benefits. For example, people can make reservations in their own language, and these language models eliminate the risk of errors that could be made by someone working at a hotel who speaks only two or maybe three languages. AI chatbots also mean that hotel staff can interact with guests in real-time and provide personalized recommendations. AI can also predict demand and adjust availability, influence pricing and inventory decisions, and reduce the overall operating costs of a hotel.

Izak: Analysts predict that the UK's AI economy will be valued at £2.4 trillion by 2027. Is this an overestimate, considering the market value now stands at $1.36 trillion?

Pranava: Well, Izak, I'm not really good at predictions. But, to answer your question, I would say yes. An increase of about £1 trillion over four years is possible. The AI market is expanding all the time and, especially now with all these cost of living issues, all businesses are looking to cut costs, and AI is one way that they can do this.

Izak: What will the role of AI be for businesses 10 years from now or even beyond this? How will this impact the UK economy? And the global economy?

Pranava: I think this goes back to what I said at the start of our chat. Businesses will continue to see AI as a tool to accelerate growth and make them more competitive. I also think AI will boost economies, including the UK, by creating more, not fewer, jobs.

Some very insightful words from Pranava that confirm much of what I have covered in this chapter. Let's end off with a prediction from one of the co-founders of ChatGPT's creator, OpenAI. You guessed it, Elon Musk. It was he who brazenly said: "I am the reason OpenAI exists."[13] That's confidence for you. But here is a closing statement from him on AI. Words, I must admit, to which we should at least take some heed.

> "I think it's very much a double-edged sword. I think… there's a strong probability that it will make life much better and that we'll have an age of abundance. There's [also] some chance that it goes wrong and destroys humanity. Hopefully, that chance is small, but it's not zero. And so, I think we want to take whatever actions we can think of to minimize the probability that AI goes wrong."[14]

Pranava Madhyastha - Senior Lecturer in Computer Science at City, University of London

Dr Pranava Madhyastha is a Senior Lecturer in Computer Science at City, University of London, where he studies multimodal machine learning models for natural language understanding and generation. His impressive resume also includes being a Research Fellow at Imperial College in London, a Visiting Scholar at the Johns Hopkins University in Baltimore, and a Research Fellow in Machine Learning at the University of Sheffield. Pranava graduated from the Polytechnic University of Catalonia in Barcelona with a PhD in Artificial Intelligence.

7

Cyber Essentials and Cyber Essentials Plus

> "When it comes to data protection, small businesses tend to be less well-prepared. They have less to invest in getting it right. They don't have compliance teams or data protection officers. But small organizations often process a lot of personal data, and the reputation and liability risks are just as real."[1]
>
> – Elizabeth Denham

Those are the words of the former UK Information Commissioner at the ICO. And what she's saying is that while SMEs don't have the cash flow like their big-spender counterparts, their cybersecurity risks are still much the same. We've spoken about applying the basics of cybersecurity and cyber hygiene and how that should keep any SME from dicing with the death of their data or IT network. But how do you know the exact state of your cyber hygiene? Is it good, bad, or somewhere in between? For SMEs in the UK, the Cyber Essentials (CE) and its bigger brother, Cyber Essentials Plus (CE+), is a means by which business owners and senior management can ascertain their level of cyber hygiene and get some peace of mind about their cybersecurity.

Let's start with the beginnings of Cyber Essentials. In the UK, more than 80% of cyber-attacks on businesses could have been prevented by implementing basic security controls.[2] To address this issue, the government introduced the Cyber Essentials Certification scheme in 2014. The scheme, run by the National Cyber Security Centre (NCSC), is a government-backed and industry-supported initiative aimed at helping businesses combat common cyber threats by implementing basic security controls. Industry support for the CE scheme was strong at launch, with backing from organizations such as the Federation of Small Businesses, the CBI, and several insurance companies that offered incentives to businesses. Since its inception, the scheme has awarded over 120,000 certificates to a range of organizations across all sectors, including businesses, charities, and educational institutions.

As of 1 October 2014, suppliers bidding for government contracts that involve handling sensitive information must be CE-certified. Ensuring the integrity of government information not only protects against potential breaches but can also provide a competitive edge when competing for public sector tenders. As such, I hope you can see why becoming certified is a big plus for SMEs and even those millions of micros out there. By obtaining certification, businesses demonstrate their commitment to cybersecurity. Although the CE scheme focuses only on the fundamentals of cybersecurity, it offers enormous benefits to those who become certified. By following the scheme's guidelines, businesses can prevent the vast majority of cyberattacks. Being CE-certified is great for SMEs wanting to improve their marketing and free cyber insurance is thrown in as an added bonus.

Cyber Essentials is not a hugely complex certification for SMEs to get. CE has five key controls that businesses need to adhere to. The first control is firewall management. By utilizing boundary firewalls and internet gateways, SMEs can control access to their system and limit users' access to specific areas. Antivirus software serves as protection against viruses and malware, while firewalls safeguard against external threats. It is possible to adjust the level of security provided by the firewall, including the "rules" governing its operation, as with other control functions. SMEs applying for CE certification need to show that they have good firewall management in place. The control also guides you to ensure that your network assets have not reach end-of-life and remain secure.

The next control is security configuration. Proper configuration of web and application servers is critical in ensuring cybersecurity. Failure to manage server configurations can lead to security disasters such as data leaks and loss, unwanted visitors to your network, and, indeed, cyberattacks. It is essential for SMEs to configure computers and network devices to minimize vulnerabilities and provide only necessary services to prevent unauthorized actions. By doing so, each device will only reveal the minimum information required to connect to the Internet. By doing so, each device will only reveal the minimum information required to the Internet. Performing scans can help identify areas of insecure configuration that can be exploited.

User access control is something that I do go on and on about and for good reason. Minimizing access to data and services is critical for cybersecurity. By doing so, unauthorized access to sensitive information can be prevented. Hackers aim to gain administrator rights to break into applications and access confidential data and providing administrator rights to multiple users for convenience makes this so much easier for them. Therefore, special access privileges and user accounts should only be assigned to authorized individuals. These accounts must be managed effectively and provide the minimum level of access required to access applications, computers, and networks.

The fourth control relates to malware. Safeguarding your business from malicious software is crucial as it can attempt to gain access to sensitive files on your system. I reiterate - malware can wreak havoc by stealing confidential information, damaging files, or denying access unless a ransom is paid. Employing measures to defend against a wide range of malware is imperative to protect your computer, your privacy, and your critical documents from malicious attacks.

Cyber Essentials and I are definitely on the same page when it comes to what you should prioritize for your security. Its fifth control is all about patch management. Put simply, technical vulnerabilities are a common weakness in all devices and software. Cybercriminals are quick to exploit any vulnerabilities that are discovered and shared publicly. Criminal hackers can exploit known vulnerabilities if operating systems and third-party applications are not properly patched or updated. Updating software and operating systems is essential to fix these known weaknesses. As I stated in earlier chapters, those who don't update are asking for it.

Getting CE certification is relatively straightforward, especially for micro-enterprises. There are four main steps to becoming CE certified. Firstly, complete the self-assessment questionnaire online at your own pace. Then, you'll need to confirm compliance of your company's IT systems with the five essential cyber security controls that we discussed. Next is to provide assurance of protection against the most common cyber-attacks to a certification body. Once you've done all these things, as a successful organisation, you'll receive a certificate and a CE branding package. Good for marketing and good for business. On average, small businesses take around two weeks to complete their CE assessment. Once the assessment is submitted, it typically takes about 3 days for the certification body to provide a response. If the assessment is satisfactory and all requirements are met, the business will be awarded the CE certification.

For those who want to go premium, there is also Cyber Essentials Plus (CE+) certification. Unlike the standard CE certification, which is on online self-assessment, the CE+ certification requires a more thorough on-premises verification in addition to the self-assessment. SMEs may find that the standard certification is sufficient for their needs, but larger businesses or those seeking to demonstrate their cybersecurity measures to clients, insurers, and professional bodies may want to consider the added assurance provided by CE+. I honestly recommend buying into the best, as this shows that you place value on your cybersecurity and cyber hygiene. It's something that won't go unnoticed, I promise. The programme is not perfect, in many ways simply providing a cyber spot check on an annual basis. While being an excellent cyber hygiene benchmark, CE still lacks the essential real-time controls needed so that we never drop the cybersecurity ball. On a positive note, CE is a work-in-progress and is evolving and improving every year. Many of our customers have become certified and they benefit from the comfort and peace that comes with the certification.

I'd now like to introduce you to a friend and associate of mine, Simon Newman, whom I recently interviewed for this chapter. Simon is a security expert and has been the CEO of the Cyber Resilience Centre for London since April 2022. He has a proven track record of successfully delivering high-profile, major business change on projects in high-risk environments both in the UK and on the international stage. This is a not-for-profit organisation with the aim of supporting SMEs in reducing their vulnerability to cybercrime. Cyber Resilience Centre for London works in partnership with the Mayor's Office for Policing and Crime. Simon has a proven track record of successfully delivering high-profile, major business change on projects in high-risk environments both in the UK and on the international stage. Let's read what Simon's take on Cyber Essentials for SMEs is.

Interview with Simon Newman

Izak: Hi Simon, great that we could spend some time talking about Cyber Essentials today. Let's start with my first question. What do you think or see as the main cyber threats and vulnerabilities facing SMEs and micros today?

Simon: [That's] a good question because the threat landscape as we see it at the moment is obviously quite broad, and organizations of all sizes are affected in lots of different ways. If we look at SMEs and micro businesses, the thing for me, and the vulnerabilities in particular, is that these organisations often fail to get the basics right. So, these are organisations that fail to implement some of those really simple control measures that don't cost anything. That will give them a significant boost to their cyber security posture. So that's things, for example, like backing up data, two-factor verification, and having a robust password policy. Really simple stuff that we expect everyone to have in place, and we assume that everyone has in place. But the reality is that they simply don't. So that, I think, is the main issue… In terms of more specific threats, ransomware seems to be a constant… I think we're also seeing that there is a growing insider threat as well. And that's not necessarily maliciously. Quite often, that's an element of carelessness, which is people perhaps not following internal processes or accidentally releasing sensitive data when they shouldn't. And part of that is about the culture of an organization not being security-focused. This means allowing these things to happen by default. So that's kind of my broad overview of what the main kinds of cyber threats and vulnerabilities are. But it really comes down to the fact that certainly, amongst those smaller organisations, it's a real failure in being able to do the really simple basic stuff properly.

Izak: Which SME industry sector or sectors do you think are the most vulnerable?

Simon: We've been trying to look at this to see whether we can find out if there are some sectors that are more vulnerable than others. And what I would say on that is, at the moment, there's a real lack of qualitative data that would support it one way or another. I mean, anyone can be a victim, and I think that's what we've got to be mindful of in this. Particularly if we look at things like supply chain attacks, which is arguably another main attack vector that has grown quite significantly in recent years. Anyone who is in a supply chain could well be a target. So, I don't think it's necessarily industry-specific at the SME level, it just seems to be anyone caught up in that attack. What I would say, though is we do know there are certain sectors that clearly have data that is understandably going to be very valuable to cybercriminals. The education sector and healthcare sector are good examples of that. But we don't have, in my view, sufficiently robust evidence to be able to point to a particular sector, location, or demographic of business that can tell us categorically, yes, this type of organisation is definitely more vulnerable than another, and why.

Izak: Simon, what would you, from your experience, say are the main challenges for SMEs and micro-enterprises in terms of getting their cybersecurity and cyber hygiene up to scratch?

Simon: I think there are quite a few challenges. One of the major issues we're seeing at the moment is people don't really understand cyber. The language that's used is often very technical. Most of the organisations don't have technical capability at that smaller end. And so, for them, it comes across as a different language. And as a result of that, people often switch off or ignore it. I think one of the challenges is getting people to understand what cyber is and how it potentially impacts their organisation. We need to do this without being too strong on the fear factor side of things. One of the other challenges I think we're seeing is in the current economic situation, clearly, the focus of many businesses post-pandemic is about survival, and things like cyber hygiene inevitably take a back seat whilst businesses try [to] keep their heads above water. I think the recent Cyber Breaches survey, which was published by the government back in March or April of this year, recognized in particular the fact that basic cyber hygiene appears to be getting worse. And I think that's really quite interesting with the government now recognizing that as well. So those are sort of two of the bigger challenges. I think another challenge as well is… where on earth they go to get advice, and this is a really big problem. So, if you engage with an SME and the SME then realises, "Okay, yeah, I've got to do something about this, where do you go?" And that's really tricky because there are lots and lots of vendors out there. Some of the vendors are very good, some of them not so good, but the customer, at the end of the day, I don't think, is particularly informed well enough to be able to make a decision on what's right for them. They need to be able to buy something that they know is tailored to their particular needs and actually will address the problems that they've got. I think there's a whole issue around the vendor community, which is a real challenge where customers effectively are going out and trying to buy solutions, [but] they're not really sure what they do or whether they work. And also, in addition to that, you know, lots of cyber solutions out there are actually pretty expensive. And when you can't really understand what it does or how it benefits your business, it's very hard to justify spending thousands of pounds on something that creates that challenge. And you may well consider that spending that money instead on another aspect of your business, potentially, is more attractive. So, I think there's a whole issue there in terms of the language around cyber, working with vendors in particular, and trying to get them to do those really simple basic things that are quite difficult. So that's kind of, I think, for me, the main challenges that we have. I'm just going to put another thing in there as well, which I think is around the messaging side. And I'm quite critical of this, but we see lots of messaging around cyber that's out there, and a lot of it, while technically very good, is not at the right level. It's either overly technical, or it uses fear. And I think that what we've missed here is trying to get underneath the thinking behind SME behaviour. So that's another big challenge. I think [what] we see is [that] we're just not being able to engage correctly with those businesses as effectively as we should be.

Izak: Okay. So, Simon, what are the benefits of Cyber Essentials and/or Cyber Essentials Plus for SMEs and very small businesses?

Simon: Cyber Essentials, obviously, is the government's standard accreditation scheme for cyber, which has been up and running now for nine years, coming into its 10th year next year. The benefit for me is that it's demonstrating to customers, staff, and suppliers that you have achieved a level of compliance against a recognized government scheme around cyber. It shows that you take data and cyber seriously, which is really good. Not just your own data but your customer's data as well. And it also, you know, I think, gives an indication of the type of quality of the organisation. Organisations that tend to go for these types of accreditations generally like to make sure they've got the right processes in place to avoid some of the challenges that we've seen. I think the other [reason] Cyber Essentials is good is that, increasingly, we're seeing it now being a requirement for tenders for contracts not just through the public sector, but now beyond that as well into the private sector. So, arguably, having Cyber Essentials can also help you win contracts to supply products and services to other organisations. So those, for me, are the two kinds of main benefits that we would have. And you know, I think increasingly it's going to become more and more required. So, it's a good thing to have in place for those organisations.

Izak: Would you say there are any obstacles to getting Cyber Essentials?

Simon: There [are] three things to me. So, one is the cost. Now, the basic accreditation obviously is scaled depending on the size of your organisation, and in principle, actually, a couple of hundred quid to get a certification doesn't seem that much, and it isn't. But what we do know is that in most cases, the SME will need some form of support and assistance to get them ready for an assessment, particularly with Cyber Essentials Plus, and that can often run into several thousands of pounds. So, suddenly, something that appears to be £300 or £400 becomes £2,000 or £3,000 very quickly. So, I think the cost element to it is one. Secondly, it's the access to that expertise to help people get to that point and the things that need to be done. We're going through Cyber Essentials Plus at the moment, actually, and although it's reasonably straightforward, I'm glad that I've got someone internally who's very,

very good cyber-wise. Otherwise, I'd have to rely incredibly heavily on an external consultant to do all of the work for us. The other challenge for me, an obstacle if you like, is the fact that Cyber Essentials is kind of a one-size-fits-all approach. And there's a particular sweet spot in terms of business size and profile that it works really well for. If you're too small, I would argue that it's possibly too much of a leap in many ways to go... perhaps as a sole trader micro business into Cyber Essentials. And as a larger organisation...some of the Cyber Essentials questions or the assessment criteria are very black and white. And a good example of that is it talks about legacy systems. Well, for larger organisations, it's almost a given as we know that they will have legacy systems in place, but they manage the risk around those legacy systems. Well, Cyber Essentials, for example, doesn't really allow you to have legacy systems, and it's a kind of a pass-fail. So, there are some things there [where] you'd like to see some greater flexibility, and I think that creates some challenges. My concern there is that Cyber Essentials is a bit of a one-size-fits-all approach, and that may be one of the reasons why there's been such a low uptake. In fact, if I were to pass comment on this, one of the issues, I think, is that most people who take Cyber Essentials do it because they're required to do so, as opposed to "I see the value in it," which I think is a cause for concern.

Izak: Is Cyber Essentials affordable? In principle, it is affordable because it's a few hundred pounds, but it's the support that may be a deterrent not so?

Simon: As I said, if you look at the basic Cyber Essentials, it's a very affordable process and relatively easy and straightforward to go through. Certainly, if you've got a degree of knowledge about what's involved. So, in some respects, it's affordable. As we said, it gets more expensive if you require specialist help. But then, of course, once you've got the certification, you've then got to ensure that you maintain compliance with it. So, there's an element of ongoing support that you might require there to continue to comply with Cyber Essentials. I think it's not a categoric yes or no in terms of affordability. Again, I think it depends on the complexity and the type of organization that's going through it.

Izak: Thanks, Simon. I'm not sure how relevant this is, but is Cyber Essentials a better option than cyber insurance, especially for SMEs?

Simon: Good question. I think they both go hand in hand. And I know if you do get Cyber Essentials, you do get free cyber insurance with it as well. I think every organisation should have cyber insurance, whether that's part of a general business insurance policy or a dedicated cyber insurance policy. I think it depends on the level of risk and the sector and [the] data that the organisation [has]. I would say both would be good to have as opposed to just one or the other.

Izak: How do you see the cyber landscape changing in the next five to ten years, and how will this impact SMEs?

Simon: First of all, if we look at the most common types of attack, then phishing remains the number one and has been for the last few years. I don't see that changing in any way because it's a very effective way that cybercriminals can target individuals and businesses at a great scale. And they can do this relatively cheaply. What I think is going to become more apparent is the use of AI. This could be things like deep fakes or generative AI like ChatGPT. We've got WormGPT now. I think we are going to see more AI-related attacks. These become more difficult for humans to spot. The example that we often use is around things like social engineering, where individuals take time to get to understand a person and then build an attack using this information - AI can do all of that much more quickly and probably much more effectively. I think it's going to be harder to spot some of these scams in the future. The other thing that I think is really interesting as well is what I mentioned earlier about the lack of basic cyber hygiene. My concern is that as the economy continues to be difficult here in the UK in the next few years, more organisations will struggle to implement basic controls. This means that their general cyber hygiene will get worse, and they will be less able to spot common cyberattacks. I worry about that, which has a knock-on impact on the economy in general, especially for SMEs. 99% of businesses in the UK are SMEs. 87% of those are micro-businesses with fewer than nine staff. It doesn't take much to knock one of these organizations offline through a cyberattack, and that has a big impact on the economy. It's good to see the recently published Risk Register from the government, again highlighting cyber as a major risk to the UK. One of the other challenges I think we face in this post-Brexit world is the ability to get the right tools. The costs of these is also an issue. There are also issues around data sharing. I think we're going through a period of a high degree of uncertainty. All we can say is that the cyber threat will certainly be there in five years and will continue to cause disruption to UK businesses.

Reflecting on Simon's words, one thing immediately jumps out at me. SMEs fail to get the basics right. Those are his words, not mine. And he's referring to everything that I highlighted in Chapters 2 and 3 of this book. That's right – from always-on security and password policies to monitoring and backups - the whole shebang. To end off, Cyber Essentials is a way for companies, and not only SMEs, to show their commitment to good cybersecurity and cyber hygiene. It's manageable and affordable, and it all starts with adhering to the basics.

Simon Newman - CEO of the Cyber Resilience Centre for London

Simon has been the CEO of the Cyber Resilience Centre for London since April 2022. He experienced senior manager with a proven track record of successfully delivering high-profile, major business change projects in high-risk environments both in the UK and internationally. Simon is well-respected for his prowess in cybersecurity, programme and project management, strategic communications, and policy. Simon was previously responsible for the Police Digital Security Centre in the UK and has held a number of senior management positions across Government, including the Home Office. Simon also worked as a Strategic Advisor to the Ministry of

8

Cyber Insurance - Stay in the Black

> "Organizations must put in place a comprehensive program – covering people, process, and technology controls – to shore up their overall cyber defenses. Until they do this, cyber insurance, as the sole mechanism to transfer and mitigate the risk, is not the right choice."[1]
>
> – Pete Bowers

That's what IT operations expert Pete Bowers has to say about cyber insurance. And I'm in agreement. Cyber insurance, or any insurance for that matter, must offer cover to match the investment in insurance. But I'm jumping the gun here. Let's start by looking at what cyber insurance is, particularly in the context of SMEs, and how they benefit from being covered.

I believe that almost every business needs cyber insurance in its IT security toolkit. As we've seen, cyberattacks are increasing at an alarming rate in the UK and beyond. As such, cyber insurance has become an increasingly popular layer of protection for businesses in all industrial sectors. This kind of coverage can help them deal with the aftermath of data breaches, security failures, or any other nasty surprises that cybercriminals might throw their way. Whether you're a small micro startup, an SME, or a big corporation, cyber insurance can help you build up your defenses and deal with the risks of the digital age. Reinsurance expert Torsten Jeworrek says:

> "Cyber insurance is fundamental for the successful digitalisation of the economy."[2]

That said, the take-up of cyber insurance is particularly low among SMEs. In the UK, only 56.2% of medium-sized businesses, 40.0% of small businesses, and 16.8% of micro-businesses had a cyber insurance policy in 2022.[3]

Going back to what we discussed with Simon in the last chapter, UK SMEs that have Cyber Essentials certification are usually eligible for cyber liability insurance from the IASME Consortium. But just because they offer it doesn't mean it's the right fit for your business. Be sure to check the details and ask questions to make sure the insurance meets your needs. As a rule of thumb, if your business has a turnover of £20 million and achieves self-assessed certification covering the whole organization to either the basic level of Cyber Essentials or the IASME Standard, you'll get a £25,000 limit of indemnity. Unfortunately, that's only enough to cover a small data breach and won't cover you for a serious problem that results in downtime, loss of revenue, reputational damage, or litigation.

Before buying cyber insurance, it's important to understand how crucial your organization's data, systems, and devices are to your operations so that you can get the right amount of coverage. Make sure you know exactly what the policy covers and what's excluded. For example, some policies won't cover losses due to business email compromise (BEC) fraud. This is just one example where a standard cyber security policy may not cover a common incident. If this is a concern for you, check that your policy covers it. Keep in mind that cyberattacks are always evolving, and you may become a victim of a new type of attack that didn't exist when you took out the policy. Check with your broker to see if you'd be covered in case of a new type of cyberattack that's not inherent to your current policy.

When you apply for cyber insurance, you'll need to be upfront about your IT security. Most insurers will require that you detail all the technical, procedural, and other aspects that keep your IT safe and sound and out of the hands of hackers. Putting that information together will probably involve speaking to your IT guys as well as everybody who handles sensitive data. For companies, including SMEs, planning on taking out a policy with a hefty premium, I often advise bringing in an external IT consultant to compile a report on their IT security. Outsourcing provides peace of mind that an expert with specialist knowledge has examined your cyber hygiene and cybersecurity. They can also advise on how to improve your security and whether you should put additional preventive measures like firewalls, antivirus software, password protections, or encryption in place. I would ask the question - are your security basics up to scratch? If the answer is yes then you're good to go and can apply for a policy or get quotes. From both a business and security standpoint, weigh up the value a particular policy will bring to your SME against the rate that the coverage ages. Remember that the cyber insurance landscape changes as quickly as that of cyber hygiene and cybersecurity.

I cannot stress enough the importance of being completely honest about your IT security. I have been a consultant to many organisations and I have sometimes seen that there is a major disconnect from what an SME says on paper to an insurer compared to the reality. While an insurer may take an application at face value, if anomalies surface at a later stage, the policy will probably be voided. Put simply, you have to be 100% accurate with all the information that you report. Most SMEs have good intentions and make mistakes by assuming they have certain cybersecurity controls in place when they don't. Assumptions pose a major risk and could lead to policies being voided, significant financial loss, and reputational damage.

You also need to establish what the most valuable IT components of your business are, your IT crown jewels, so to speak. You need to imagine the worst-case scenarios and disasters your SME simply couldn't afford should they befall you. Don't just settle for the bare minimum security standards that your insurance company wants you to follow. You need to take a close look at your existing IT security and make sure you're protecting what matters most to you. Cyber insurance is much more than securing your data and your IT. It also means securing the future of your business.

One aspect of applying for cyber insurance that I question is the ability to go online and take out a policy in minutes. There's no way that a reputable insurer can determine the state of an SME's cybersecurity based on the analysis of an online questionnaire, particularly those of the check-box variety. They are also unable to advise on any mitigative or remedial steps that should be taken. My concerns are echoed by Phillip Harris, the Research Director of IDC, the Massachusetts-headquartered global market intelligence firm. He says:

> "The cyber insurers that require customers to fill out their cybersecurity questionnaire are ultimately only getting a limited, point-in-time view of the insured security posture. Companies that have not had a professional cybersecurity services vendor complete a detailed assessment to have a complete picture of deficiencies, plans to remediate, and an ongoing roadmap for improvement are doing themselves a disservice by depending upon a somewhat generalized security questionnaire."[4]

Unless insurers have a specialist cybersecurity team in place, they should stick to doing what they know best - underwriting. As I mentioned earlier, a qualified cybersecurity vendor can supply a detailed risk assessment. Using this, the insurer is then in a position to make a sound judgment call on which policy to offer an SME. Often, SMEs then benefit from lower premiums and a policy that fits their exact cybersecurity needs.

So, what will your policy cover? Good question. This depends on your insurer and the type of cyber insurance policy that you take out. First-party coverage typically includes direct costs incurred by your business as a result of cybercrime. Usually, your insurer will cover investigating a cybercrime, where experts are paid to help you find the source of the cybercrime that affected your business. You should also be able to hire legal experts to advise you about any regulations you need to comply with regarding a breach. The insurer should also pay for you to bring in IT experts to repair and restore data, software, and computer systems damaged in a cyberattack.

From a business operations perspective, a creditable insurer should also cover reputation damage and management. This could involve covering the costs of a public relations campaign to repair your reputation and paying for free credit monitoring services or credit protection services for affected customers. And what if an attack or breach temporarily prevents you from doing business? A good provider will cover loss of revenue and should also cough up for notification costs, covering the cost of notifying affected third parties, such as your customers and suppliers, of a data breach or ransomware attack.

If you take out third-party insurance, you'll be covered for the indirect dramas following a cyberattack. If your SME offers professional services to other companies and you get sued because an attack has resulted in damage, the third-party cover will ensure that you don't go into the red by paying litigation costs and penalties. Third-party insurance will, however, set you back more than the cover that only protects your SME against the direct consequences of a cyberattack.

You should know that cyber insurance generally does not cover property damage, which includes computer and other technology equipment that is often damaged as part of the cyberattack. This can be problematic if the hardware configuration has become so corrupt that its reconfiguration would be expensive and take a lot of time. In this case, it might be more cost-efficient to purchase or migrate to a new solution.

Now let's reflect again for a minute on the words of Pete Bowers:

> "Organizations must put in place a comprehensive program – covering people, process, and technology controls – to shore up their overall cyber defenses."[5]

Any cyber insurance vendor worth their salt should go above and beyond covering you after the event. Prevention is always better than cure, and your insurer should take on some responsibility for IT forensics, including managing your cyber risk and providing advice on effective access control, protection, monitoring, and incident reporting. Your insurer could also be involved in staff training and advising on which trusted partners and suppliers to use. Some insurers have their own in-house cyber incident response team that can give you guidance on incident management to help you plan and build an effective cyber incident response capability. Also, as your business and IT scale, so should your cyber insurance. Your policy must be flexible enough to accommodate scaling your SME.

And now the question that everybody asks - how much will it cost me? This will depend on which vendor you use and the extent of cover. Other factors insurers consider are the size of a business, the amount and sensitivity of the data you handle, and obviously, the strength of your cybersecurity. The industry sector you operate in will also come into play. SMEs in finance, retail, manufacturing, or healthcare, for example, are much more prone to cyberattacks than those in hospitality.

Speaking of the healthcare industry, let's take a trip across the pond to the United States for a moment. In June 2023, a significant data breach occurred at one of the largest Medicaid and CHIP dental care providers in North America, Managed Care of North America (MCNA) Dental.

The breach exposed highly sensitive patient information, including Social Security numbers, care records, information about treatment visits, insurance claims, and other identifying details along with complete personal contact information. The breach, executed by the LockBit ransomware group, affected a total of 8,923,662 individuals. Although the healthcare sector has not traditionally been a primary target, major groups like LockBit and its affiliates have increasingly focused on it in the past year or two. Patient care facilities typically lack substantial cash reserves to meet ransom demands, but the attackers may anticipate a potential insurance payout, given the industry's inability to withstand even moments of downtime. With this example in mind, the healthcare sector in the States is subject to much higher cyber insurance premiums than other industries due to the sensitive nature of the data used. It is highly likely that the UK will soon follow suit.

So, going back to the actual cost in pounds and pence. A ballpark number is in the range of £10 to £15 per user, but it will also depend on all the factors I've mentioned. Also, shop around. Book an appointment online, sure. But then see your insurer, preferably face-to-face or via video, so you can explain your needs and negotiate a good premium. You are the customer, after all.

There are also two components to the cost - the insurance premium and the insurance excess. This is the standard for most insurance policies. The premium you can pay annually or monthly by direct debit. Paying yearly will generally save you money. The excess, like any other insurance policy, is a lump sum you need to pay when you make a claim. If you choose a small excess, this will usually push up your premium.

Most cyber insurance policies are checked every year, so it's up to you to keep your cybersecurity details accurate and up-to-date. Insurers need to know what kind of security measures you've got in place and any other relevant information. If your situation changes, like adding new tech or software, you need to let your insurer know so you stay covered. If you tell your insurer that you've got security measures in place when you haven't, it's likely that your policy will be voided, and they won't pay out any claims should disaster strike. Honesty is the best policy, so always be upfront about your cybersecurity.

Ransomware has also had a massive impact on cyber insurance. IBM says that the average ransomware payment is around £700,000 for companies who opt to pay the ransom.[6] That said, in June 2021, the meat-processing vendor, JSA USA, was hit by an attack and reportedly paid $11 million in ransom to criminals that were using the REvil ransomware. Insurers can be wary about covering ransomware or might offer it at a premium price. Josephine Wolff, a Professor of Cybersecurity Policy at Tufts University in Massachusetts, says this of the rise in ransomware and its impact on cyber insurance:

> "I think the insurers are still figuring out, 'How confident are we in our ability to estimate and predict this risk?' Policyholders started filing a lot more ransom claims, and the insurers were making a lot less money – and they were worried that they would even start losing money. I definitely think that having insurance coverage for ransom payments changes the calculus for companies deciding whether or not to pay. It's the difference between, 'Am I going to be out of this money myself, or am I going to file a claim with my insurer and have them cover most or all of it?'"[7]

Fearmongers out there will say that SMEs are getting priced out of cyber insurance. This is not true. With the global cyber insurance market predicted to be valued at $85 billion by 2030, there will always be insurers who will take SMEs under their wing.

I'm dedicating the rest of this chapter to gleaning the crown jewels of London Insurance Market professional, Roger Oldham. Roger has over 35 years of experience in the London and international insurance markets at a senior level. He is the founder and MD of the market networking and thought leadership hub, LMF - London Market Forums. At LMF, Roger hosts a Cyber Insurance Industry Practice Group, comprising brokers and underwriters who come together to discuss the development of this class of insurance. Here's Roger's advice on cyber insurance for SMEs.

Interview with Roger Oldham

Izak: Hi Roger. Thanks for your time today. Let's start off with something quite broad. Why is cyber insurance an important part of cybersecurity, especially for small businesses?

Roger: I think mostly because of the support system that comes along with cyber insurance, the extent to which will depend on the policy coverage you've purchased. When you invest in a cyber insurance policy, you are getting more than just a risk transfer mechanism. It's more than just ringing up a number and trying to get some kind of compensation or indemnity for the loss that you've suffered. When you have a cyber incident, you'll naturally want assistance as soon as possible. Cyber insurance will often incorporate a range of services and support systems. Depending on which route you go down, whether it's broking through a broker or you go directly to an insurer, you are going to get complete service on the whole – depending on where you go, of course. There's a big range. Some companies will provide a truly comprehensive service and policy of indemnity, helping you from risk identification and quantification, through to a breach when it happens, as well as the recovery process and getting you back on your feet. Cyber Insurance can be about provide a total support mechanism that's more than just a policy of indemnity, depending on the type of service/policy you purchase. Policyholders should take time to really understand their own policy, the services offered and the terms and conditions. If in doubt, they should seek clarification from their broker or intermediary. This is why cyber insurance is important when it comes to SMEs. That whole area of cyber resilience is extraordinarily dynamic, and cyber insurers don't work in isolation. They work in partnership with cybersecurity companies, IT firms, infosec organisations, law firms and subject matter experts from around the world to provide that complete basket of solutions and services.

Izak: Great. What would you say are the benefits of having cyber insurance? I know that you touched on this already.

Roger: I think the number one benefit is that an SME will then have a support network if their policy extends to provide such services. Once you've got that support mechanism in place, you've got somewhere to go when something happens. It is a fact that there is very little support for a company that is suffering from some form of cyber incident or breach. There's very little support outside of your own contractual arrangements with suppliers, infosec staff, or whatever you've set up. You can't really go to the government and say that you've suffered a cybersecurity incident and ask for help. They are unlikely to have the capacity, mechanism or infrastructure to provide local support when you need it the most. They might give you some high-level advice or you might be able to go to a Cyber Resilience Centre like the one in London, who are very helpful. So going back to the main benefit. If you're a small business, and your policy provides certain support services or extensions to coverage, you may be able to pick up the phone and say I'm concerned about this, I think I might be the victim of a cyber breach. Within a short time, the relevant expert from the cyber insurer's panel of service providers should be able to provide you with a comforting response or at least direction.

Izak: Is cyber insurance affordable for the average SME, especially with the current cost of living crisis where many are struggling to make ends meet?

Roger: You should be able to find a policy that's affordable. I think what you have to do is find a policy that fits your own company's needs. Some people will want very comprehensive coverage that will cover the whole digital ecosystem and some will want lesser coverage. Some policyholders will find that there is a degree of cyber cover under their existing commercial insurance policy – potentially there will be some cyber insurance included in their normal commercial combined business cover. Every policy is different but if a company is looking for comprehensive cyber insurance protection, they'll have to extend their existing policy to cover that or buy a standalone cyber insurance policy. Cyber insurance is changing quite a lot so some of the new companies that have emerged in the last three to five years don't offer just conventional cyber insurance. They offer a complete, holistic range of services, including education and training. So, I think in terms of affordability, you have to decide on the extent to which you want a support service and a policy of indemnity and then find something that works for you. There are policies out there that are very economical and there are those that are more expensive but provide more coverage. I'd like to add that the loss ratios for some insurers in this class of insurance business has been fairly high because we are living in a very dynamic risk environment. Therefore, in terms of pricing, the costs of policies will always be impacted by loss ratios. How much are they paying out in claims? How much are they bringing in in premiums? If there's a discrepancy, they'll correct that by way of higher premiums or coverage changes. I think it's something to watch as insurance premiums for cyber are likely to go up because claims, particularly ransomware claims, are going up. It's essential that all policyholders really understand their obligations, along with warranties, subjectivities and exclusions, under any policy of insurance and that includes cyber insurance.

Izak: What happens if a business has Cyber Essentials certification? They automatically get cover of £25,000. Is that enough cover?

Roger: Cyber Essentials is a good hygiene process. It's one of the tools that can be used to help a firm protect itself. It is piece in the jigsaw puzzle. It helps firms and their staff to become aware of cyber risk and exposures. However, it is in no way deemed to be a suitable replacement for cyber insurance. Depending on the cyber insurance coverage you buy, it provides much more and Cyber Essentials isn't going to be there to answer the telephone when you have a breach, which unfortunately, many of us will incur at some stage. This is an inevitability of running an organisation. It may not be a heavily targeted attack. It could just be an innocent phishing email that starts off a chain reaction that causes malware to enter the ecosystem of the company. Before you know it, you've got a problem on your hands.

Izak: How do SMEs know that they're getting a good deal? Do they shop around?

Roger: There are various ways of doing this for an SME. They need to consider what is best for them and many SMEs these days buy their insurance directly from an insurer – not all will, though. Some of the older and more established SMEs may well have worked with a broker for many years and will continue to do so. That broker will do a fantastic job in finding them the best cover. There are a lot of new insurers on the market that offer these more comprehensive cyber coverages. They will work directly with SMEs as opposed to brokers. If an SME isn't an expert in the area of information security – and let's face it, most of us aren't - using a broker or intermediary of some sort is definitely an advisable step. This will ensure that they get the best coverage with the appropriate insurer and they get support from the broker. Many of the brokers have invested heavily in enhancing their cyber practices to provide their clients with a lot of support and advice. My advice is that if somebody isn't wholly confident, they should use an intermediary like a broker.

Izak: Roger, which are the most vulnerable sectors?

Roger: Any business that is holding sensitive data is particularly vulnerable. But I would go as far as to say that any business now has a vulnerability to cyberattacks or cyber breaches. Any organisation that is holding personal data that can be sold or held to ransom will be higher on the list for criminals. However, the disruption effect of a cyber incident can be as damaging as anything else. There are stories of petrol stations owned by one person with two or three stations. They have an attack that brings down their computer systems. Their impact on the loss of trade is significant – not only from the data that they might or might not hold but from the loss of business. Business interruption is a very big component of the cyber insurance picture.

Izak: Are there any challenges for SMEs when they want to take out a cyber insurance policy?

Roger: The cyber insurance market is fairly new – only about 20 years old. Marine insurance has been going for 350 years here in the United Kingdom and is a very well-established and well-understood class of business. Cyber is very different. We don't have the volumes of data on which to base decisions, and we're also working in a very dynamic and changing environment where the risks are changing on a frequent basis. The nature of the risk is changing as is the origin. So, it's a challenge for SMEs in some ways because when they go to an insurer, they will be asked questions. Many insurers will ask different sets of questions. There are some standard questions that tend to get asked, but I expect what we'll see is increasing layers of questioning and risk assessment, as we go along this journey. The levels of digital security that firms will have to have are only going to increase in order to meet the underwriting requirements of insurers. That's why we've seen this explosion in cybersecurity companies offering a whole range of products and services that can support those businesses – not just big ones but the SMEs as well. It's an evolving situation and there isn't a standard set of questions. That's why using a broker who can judge whether the questions being asked are reasonable is so valuable. They might even be able to assist in the collection of the required data.

Izak: What is the UK government's stance, if any, on cyber insurance?

Roger: The UK government believes that cyber insurance is a valuable tool in the armoury of any organisation. The UK government gives certain advice about handling cyber incidents. For example, the UK government does not support the payment of ransomware. That's not to say that they are not paid by either the organisation or the insurers, but the UK government does not openly support this. I think the government's stance is that cyber insurance plays a very important role and the firms should use as many tools as are available to them to help build up those layers of protection. That's why there's been investment in Cyber Resilience Centres which are playing a very important role all around the United Kingdom. No organisation should say I've got cyber insurance and therefore I'm protected. Some companies think because they purchase cyber insurance they don't have to worry. That's not the case. It is the duty of all companies and all individuals to be as secure as possible and to make their infrastructure as secure as possible. Cyber insurance isn't the silver bullet.

Izak: Thanks, Roger. Just to wind up, is there anything you'd like to add as to how you perceive cyber insurance in the future?

Roger: Cyber insurance is going to grow, that's for sure. As I said earlier, it's still relatively new but is becoming more sophisticated as time goes on. There are more and more people entering the cyber insurance environment. The best thing you could do is probably research the latest statistics on the volume, percentage-wise, of companies that procure cyber insurance and where that's looking to go. There's some very good data out there that shows the projected trends in procuring cyber insurance. There's going to be massive growth in cyber insurance. I think we'll all be buying cyber insurance – individuals and companies. The range of services that the insurers are offering as part of the packages will certainly assist with good cyber hygiene in organizations. That's why it isn't necessarily the right thing for a company to think because they've ticked the box by buying cyber insurance and everything is rosy. That's not the thing. As a business owner, you've got to be constantly on your guard. As we know one of the biggest areas of weakness in any business is staff inadvertently clicking on something in an email, for example. That being said, as one person told me, it's the owners of the business and management that have a responsibility for cyber security, and this shouldn't reside with the employees. That being said, employee awareness of the dangers is a powerful tool That's why firms are spending vast amounts of money on training their staff to be as aware as possible – including insurance companies. I think training and awareness will become as important as anything else when it comes to cyber hygiene and security awareness.

At the end of the day, remember that cyber insurance won't stop a cyberattack. As Roger wisely said, it isn't the silver bullet. Only cybersecurity and sticking to the basics can do that. And when we think about the speed, sophistication, and evolving nature of cybercrime, I know it isn't a question of *if it happens* but rather *when it happens*. In that case, it's much better to be safe than sorry. Put simply, enforce good cyber hygiene and cybersecurity and have cyber insurance in your arsenal as a backup to lean on. Although I fully support companies taking out cyber insurance, it shouldn't lull them into a false sense of security over their cybersecurity – forgive the pun! Cyber insurance shouldn't give us the excuse to become careless. Any SME applying for cyber insurance needs to honest and transparent about their IT – with the insurer and themselves. And remember that any pre-insurance assessment is almost a box-ticking exercise. It does not reflect the status quo of an SME's IT in real time.

Roger A. Oldham - Founder and Managing Director at London Market Forums (LMF) and experienced insurance industry adviser.

Roger has over 35 years frontline experience in the London and international insurance markets at executive level. He is known for founding and running the successful market networking and thought leadership hub, LMF - London Market Forums. The group brings thousands of professionals together every year and is free to access for all insurance professionals. Roger is also an experienced and qualified mediator, having trained with the Chartered Institute of Arbitrators in London. During his career, Roger has been responsible for functions and teams at firms such as Aon, HSBC and Marsh. He has led claims teams, multi-region operations and change projects in the Middle East, Far East and North America.

9

Online Fraud Threats—Penny Wise Pound Foolish

> "Fraud really thrives in moments of great social change and transition. We're in the midst of a technological revolution. That gives con artists huge opportunities. People lose their frame of reference for what can and can't be real."[1]
>
> – Maria Konnikova

I think Russian-American writer Maria Konnikova has hit the nail on the head with her description of fraud in our day and age. As she aptly says, threat actors take advantage of us vulnerable humans during times of change. And as we know, technological change is moving at a rate that nobody ever anticipated. Directly linked to this phenomenal growth is a blossoming online fraud industry. With the internet at the centre of our lives, there are many kinds of fraud to go along with it, such as identity theft, fake online transactions, including those involving cryptocurrency, dating and other scams, spam, spyware, identity theft, phishing, and other forms of social engineering like scareware and pretexting. All these are designed with one thing in mind - to fool you and take your money, your identity, or both.

Barclays said recently that 77% of scams now originate from social media, online marketplaces, and dating apps, with a huge spike in fraud cases on Meta-owned Facebook and WhatsApp. Fake listings on Facebook Marketplace have doubled in a year, while impersonation scams on WhatsApp have tripled.[2] In August 2023, a former City of London worker, let's call her Jane Doe for simplicity, discovered that her Facebook account had been hacked by malicious individuals. They illicitly employed her stored credit card information to finance various online advertisements, including online gambling and Halloween costumes. The crooks initiated a nominal charge of only £1 on her credit card. Additionally, they established a payment schedule that could have resulted in daily charges of up to £5,000 for the advertisements. Fortunately for Jane, her bank was expedient in freezing her account. She was unable to contact Meta as she had been locked out of her account. Action Fraud, a hotline run by the City of London Police, was finding it increasingly difficult to tackle the wave of reported social media scams and could only assign a case officer in 28 days.[3] All of this makes me pose the question - how are victims of online fraud supposed to get the protection that they deserve? A spokesperson from Meta had this to say:

> "We don't want anyone to fall victim to these criminals, which is why our platforms have systems to block scams, financial services advertisers now have to be FCA (Financial Conduct Authority)–authorized and we run consumer awareness campaigns on how to spot fraudulent behaviour."[4]

Jane Doe's case clearly shows us that even the IT experts at these social media giants are in the dark when it comes to curbing online fraud. And as for running consumer awareness campaigns? I think you all know where I stand on cybersecurity training by now. As a reminder – I think it only works 5% of the time. People will continue to make mistakes, no matter how much cyber education they have. The only way to prevent online fraud is to ensure people don't become victims.

According to the UK bank TSB, approximately 60% of purchase fraud incidents, where scammers deceive buyers by selling items they never intend to deliver, occur on Facebook Marketplace. On top of this, around two-thirds of impersonation fraud cases are currently taking place on WhatsApp.[5] Liz Ziegler, Lloyds Banking fraud prevention director, believes that the financial sector is facing an epidemic of social engineering scams and says:

> "With more than 70% of fraud starting with contact through the main tech platforms, these companies must be held responsible for stopping scams at source and putting things right for innocent victims."[6]

The National Crime Agency (NCA) also paints a sad picture of online fraud in the UK. In 2022, there were 3.7 million incidents of fraud costing individuals and businesses, including SMEs, £2.5 billion, a 17% increase on the previous year.[7] It's also thought that about 86% of fraud instances are underreported. In the UK, 78% of authorized push payment (APP) fraud cases - those that happen when someone is tricked into sending money to a fraudster posing as a genuine payee - started online and resulted in losses for businesses and individuals totalling £485 million in 2022.[8] Only 25% of fraud cases originate through email.[9]

Daniel Holmes, a fraud prevention leader and former digital fraud manager at Lloyds, says:

> "Rapid changes in technology bring us to a new and critical inflection point in the fraud space. The risks remain elevated as fraudsters adapt and use increasingly sophisticated tactics and technology to fool consumers."[10]

And by consumers, I don't think that Daniel is only referring to online shoppers. I believe that he means all of us who access the Internet.

So, how exactly do these guys commit online fraud? We know all about using social media platforms and social engineering, as well as deepfake synthetic identity fraud. The UK Metropolitan Police goes so far as to say that online fraud and cybercrime are tantamount to the same thing. It is fraud that takes place online, committed using computers and assisted by online technology.[11] What is also a worry is that online fraud has become much faster thanks to real-time payments and the ability to convert funds to crypto and then launder them through fake online bank accounts. Typically, though, online fraud victims either fall for email and text scams or social engineering manipulation or not being able to differentiate between a fake website and the real deal.

You've already seen that online fraud in the UK costs businesses and individuals almost £500 million every year. From the very personal perspective of those who experienced financial losses due to various scams, 42% lost an amount ranging from £1 to £99, and 21% reported losing £1,000 or more.[12] Here, two people reflect on being taken for a ride by a scam. First, we hear from Jane Doe about an investment scam, and then John Doe tells us about a cryptocurrency scam that he was taken in by.

> "I was looking for a place to get interest on my savings and saw a lovely website and dashboard of investment results. The company was responsive and charming and they had great customer service…[it] seemed too good to be true… [I was] sucked into it, so [I] put all my savings into it…we don't understand what happened to us."[13]
>
> "Reality dawned on me the next day and I'd lost £31K…depressed for a couple of days and didn't go to work…it's like losing a loved one…you don't get over it but learn to live with it."[14]

Two things that Jane and John said really jump out at me. First off, when it seems too good to be true, it probably isn't good at all. So go with your instinct and gut feeling. John added that we don't get over an online scam. A minor loss - no problem. But £31,000 gone to crypto scammers? That's a depressing thought, if any.

The impact of online fraud on businesses, including SMEs, is wide-ranging. Businesses incur financial losses from both fraudulent disputes and their efforts to prevent fraud from happening in the first place. When a business loses a dispute, it becomes liable for more than just the initial transaction amount. Fraudulent activities frequently result in chargeback fees. These are expenses linked to the bank reversing the card payment and increased network fees due to disputes. The impact of fraud on businesses extends beyond mere monetary losses. Many find themselves compelled to expand their fraud prevention teams or redirect their product and engineering resources to handle operational burdens, diverting valuable assets and resources from their primary product focus.

Fraud prevention can be a costly affair. That's why companies try to pass the buck and responsibility onto social media and other tech giants. To be honest, the digital landscape is diverse, with many opportunities for fraudulent activities at different stages. When we think about the complexity of our online world, why should banks bear the exclusive burden of responsibility for online fraud prevention? The reality is that holding banks solely accountable for online fraud would be an outdated, one-dimensional solution to a contemporary, digitally progressive challenge.

Identifying and avoiding being a victim of online fraud is much like what I've been hammering home in this book so far. Don't over-complicate things. Hackers aren't complicated beasts, so simply stick to the basics, and you'll outfox them. These basics include identifying phishing, social engineering, and dodgy websites.

To safeguard yourself against phishing scams, I advise all of these precautions. Don't open attachments or click links in emails or texts from unfamiliar or unknown sources. Never disclose your personal information, financial data, or passwords in response to unsolicited emails, unexpected phone calls, or text messages. Use email security for all your accounts. And this one might be a bit old school, but it works - when you log into an account, always directly type the website address yourself to access it. Also, use the MFA approach and always call back on the number you are given for verification. By implementing these measures, you can bolster your defences and minimise the risk of cyber fraud impacting you or your business.

Social networking is cool, but as we know, once something is out there, it's out there for good. It's out of your control. As Erica Albright says in the 2010 movie The Social Network:

> "The Internet's not written in pencil, Mark, it's written in ink."[15]

To reduce the chance of online fraud on social platforms, I strongly recommend these things. Make sure your privacy settings are set to the max and review them regularly, as updates may impact your settings. I would also advise against accepting friend requests - or the equivalent for whatever platform you're using - from people you don't know. Whenever feasible, block applications and social media platforms from tracking and displaying your location to prevent unknown individuals from following you. As I said, once it's out there, there is no getting it back, so exercise caution when sharing images, videos, and content online. Keep in mind that if you wouldn't say or do something in the real world, it's best not to engage in it online.

You'll remember that Jane Doe thought an offer was too good to be true. So don't fall for fake websites. Usually, you can spot them from a mile away. Scrutinize the domain name for authenticity and check spelling and grammar on web pages. Does the URL look authentic? For example, Netflix will always be Netflix.com, not Netflix.co.uk or anything else. Are the prices of goods and services on offer unrealistically low? I would also avoid making payments via bank transfer. Legitimate websites typically accept standard payment methods like credit and debit cards and PayPal. If you have the time, read through the terms, conditions, and policies to ensure they are transparent and fair.

In 2022, British consumers set a new spending record of £9.42 billion during the Black Friday weekend, with 61% of this expenditure occurring online. Black Friday, or what has now become Cyber Week, is a time when you should be especially vigilant online. In the United States, Black Friday originates from the idea that businesses operate in a financial deficit, often referred to as being "in the red," until the day following Thanksgiving. On this day, extensive sales events finally enable them to achieve profitability, figuratively putting them "in the black." The one thing you don't want is to be in the red after Cyber Week. The typical scams you should watch out for are fake websites, fake orders, fake delivery notifications and gift card scams. Always check before you buy and confirm the legitimacy of the company you're dealing with. Watch out for fake websites with tell-tale signs of unusual design elements and functional glitches, such as broken links, typos, and slow-loading pages. I also recommend that you use credit rather than debit cards. In the UK, when you use your credit card to make a purchase between £100 and £30,000, you're protected by 'section 75' of the Consumer Credit Act. This provision means that the credit card company shares equal responsibility or liability in case of fraud. And finally, my golden rule – never, ever click unfamiliar links. Remember, nothing is too good to be true!

Businesses should also remain especially vigilant and be on the lookout for fake or counterfeit invoices. Fake invoice scams are those in which attackers send emails to their victims, masquerading as bills or invoices. These emails don't contain harmful attachments or even phishing links. Instead, they solely feature a toll-free telephone number. You are requested to contact the criminals via phone, and they instruct you to visit a URL - a malicious one, at that. Fraudsters often send an invoice from a company you deal with and rely on you to act quickly to pay any outstanding amount. Chester Wisniewski, a principal research scientist at SOPHOS, explains how vulnerabilities in email services are in part responsible for fake invoice scams:

> "Email providers all have reasonably good filtering for keeping this stuff out of your mailbox when there's a file attached that's really dangerous. But if they can convince you to go out and retrieve the dangerous thing, they're getting around the email filter."[16]

Bogdan Botezatu, Director of Threat Research at Bitdefender, cautioned that amidst the various methods scammers employ to target businesses, spam emails continue to be the most widespread. Referring to statistics from June 2020 to 2021, he said:

> "We have observed that approximately 96% of global email traffic constituted spam."[17]

Botezatu further clarified that a significant portion of this spam comprised commercial content, which, while annoying, was harmless. Among the malicious spam, phishing messages emerged as the most prevalent type. If you think an email is suspicious, check the email address for any anomalies. Also, fake parties could be copied into the email to add authenticity and authority to a request. Inspect email addresses of copied parties just as carefully as the sender's email. Also watch out for a different tone. You should check vocabulary, spelling, grammar, and sentence construction, as errors in these are definitely red flags. Does the email have a sense of urgency? That's an attempt to make you react. Don't!

Whether you're aiming to seize the most enticing Prime Day or Black Friday Week bargains, stay updated on the latest developments in the Ukraine War, or ensure you pay your taxes on time, scammers have sneakily harnessed the internet's pervasive presence in our daily lives. They are nimble and can swiftly adapt their tactics. For example, exploiting people's empathy is a time-tested strategy for scammers. In 2021, the FTC (Federal Trade Commission) reported the closure of a robocall charity scam that targeted 67 million individuals. Over the span of a decade and more than 1 billion robocalls, the bad guys managed to amass a staggering $110 million in fraudulent donations.[18] This rather sad complaint to the FTC paints the true picture of just how devastating online fraud can be:

> "Defendants knowingly duped generous Americans into donating tens of millions of dollars to nonprofit organizations that they claimed helped breast cancer patients, the families of children with cancer, homeless veterans, fire victims, and more. In reality, almost no money went to the charitable purposes the Defendants described to donors."[19]

The long and the short is that online fraud is with us, and everyone online is at risk. But there is a lot you can do to protect yourself. Fraudsters will send out a barrage of messages to as many people as possible to up their odds of hitting the jackpot. If you become a victim of fraud, there may be nothing or very little the police can do to help, especially if the incident is online. The onus is on you to protect yourself. If your inbox is overflowing with emails from one company or person, be wary - it might be a scam. Don't let them toy with your feelings. Stay alert. Verify information before doing anything. Use security tools to fend off dangerous websites and spam messages. Do these things, and you'll be able to enjoy the internet and work without worry.

10

Remote Working—Stay Secure Out and About

> "The pandemic has stretched companies' networks, accelerated their digital transformation and exposed them to more cyber-crime. Cybersecurity has never been more important."[1]
>
> – Mike Azzara

Veteran business technology and media intrapreneur Mike Azzara has strong feelings about the impact of the pandemic on cybersecurity, and so do I. The unexpected and rapid arrival of the coronavirus caused the perfect storm and meant that millions of employees around the planet had no option but to work from home (WFH). In the UK, at the height of the first wave of the coronavirus pandemic, in April 2020, 47% of workers were working out of their digs, and just 31% were commuting to work.[2] [3] What did that mean in terms of cybersecurity and staying secure online?

I think it was the perfect storm, making us more vulnerable to cybercrime than ever before. Employees from businesses of all sizes flocked in droves into the world of WFH with no notice to work remotely, unarmed, and with no cyber defenses. Millions of workers were out on a limb and vulnerable to cyberattacks, especially those with no or limited IT security knowledge. Many were accessing sensitive data on company networks using unsecured BYODs. To make matters even worse, businesses did not have enough notice or time to conduct a thorough remote working security assessment. That was the sad reality. Fortunately, four years down the line, we have adapted to a new and more secure way of remote working although many are still not sticking to the basics and are taking short cuts.

To give you an idea of the increased cyber threat caused by the pandemic, let's check out some stats from the Swiss National Cyber Security Centre. The governmental technical authority reported that in April 2020, there were 350 cyberattacks in Switzerland. This was well above the average of around 100 to 150.[4] The incidents ranged from phishing to DDoS and attacks using fraudulent websites, including a high-profile attempt to extort $6 million from the Swiss train manufacturer Stadler by hackers who stole business documents. This spike in cyberattacks was blamed on the lack of internet security that WFH individuals had. Overall, one in seven workers said that they had experienced a cyberattack during the pandemic period.[5]

Another rather alarming revelation is that approximately 47% of home workers fall for phishing scams and click on dubious links in emails.[6] We all know where that can lead. In the first few months of 2020, Phishing emails spiked by over 600%, and cloud-based attacks increased by 630%.[7] Hackers took advantage of people's fears, uncertainties, and stress during the pandemic, and Google reported that it recorded 18 million daily email scams related to COVID-19 in a single week.[8] It was also reported that 30 scam websites posed as the real thing – either official government website or healthcare providers - collecting personal data and credit card numbers. With over 40,000 domain names using the word *coronavirus*, users had to be on full alert. Many people reported that stress and confusion were the root causes of all the mistake-making.

During the pandemic, remote workers faced a barrage of over 100,000 phishing attacks within four months, mostly involving Google-branded websites, according to a report by Barracuda Networks.[9] The attacks applied spear phishing by impersonating legitimate websites to trick users into disclosing login credentials. Google-branded sites accounted for about 65,000 of the attacks, making up 65% of the attacks experienced during the study, while Microsoft-branded impersonation attacks accounted for just 13% of the attacks reported between 1 January and 30 April 2020.[10]

Previously unseen malware attacks were 20% of cyberattacks pre-pandemic. During the pandemic, this increased to 35%.[11] On British soil, the City of London Police reported in July 2020 that more than £11 million had been lost due to COVID-19 scams since January of that year. There were 2,866 victims of coronavirus-related scams and 13,820 reports of coronavirus-related phishing emails.[12] That's a lot of money and many victims in only six months.

Besides playing on people's emotions and weaknesses, how were hackers able to gain this incredible advantage? Typically, home networks are insecure, devices are shared for personal use, and Wi-Fi can be overwhelmed with VPN traffic. Residential internet service is not, by design, made for an entire workforce to work from home because of limited bandwidth. Furthermore, business VPNs have overloaded many systems that had not been tested and ready for everyone to work from home. Bryan Hamman, the Regional Director at NetScout, tells us why the pandemic was a heyday for cybercriminals:

> "Cybercriminals have been given a golden opportunity to take advantage of the global COVID-19 pandemic to launch attacks on people working from home, as companies try their utmost to keep their organizations operational."[13]

Remote working and WFH are still very much with us. Even though we might think we are through the storm, we still need to continue to apply best practises. This is the only way to manage major increase in security threats we are seeing today. More than ever before, we need to ensure we are properly equipped.

Almost 20,000 new coronavirus-related domains have been registered since the end of April 2020, and 17% of those were malicious or suspicious.[14] Impersonating popular video conferencing apps like Zoom and Microsoft Teams became a popular choice for cybercriminals, often using phishing to get the victim to click on a link that either delivers malware or tricks the user into revealing sensitive information.

Let's talk about Zoom bombing for a minute. About 230 Pasco County parents in Florida tuned in to a Zoom meeting on the evening of 11 June 2020 to hear the school superintendent, Kurt Browning, talk about plans to return to campus in August. Suddenly, a stream of new participants poured into the call, which organizer Denise Nicholas said was supposed to be on a paid secure version of Zoom. The uninvited "guests" weren't interested in whether Pasco County schools would be using a split-day schedule or online education. Instead, they spouted racist rantings while taking over the screen with pornographic images. Nicholas quickly shut the meeting down and reported the incident to Zoom.[15] But the writing had been on the wall. Between January and

May 2020, a total of 6,576 Zoom-related domains were registered globally, many of which were suspicious or malicious.[16] A major impact on businesses of Zoom bombing is that it can lead to hefty fines for any sensitive data breaches and data loss, but there also is irreparable reputation damage and one out of five businesses in the UK is forced to close after a cyberattack.[17]

So how exactly do we keep ourselves secure when working remotely, especially because for many of us, this was or is the first time? Remember that attacks occur across a range of channels, including the cloud, smartphones, and the e-commerce ecosystem. Organisations need a security solution that is robust and operates across these channels if they hope to create the most secure possible experience for their staff, customers, and sensitive data. But staying safe and secure when working from home really just boils down to the basics. This is what I tell employees of the SMEs that we work with.

Cybersecurity training helps to make people aware and on their guard against threats. Encourage your staff to attend any awareness training that your company provides. If your organisation does not have such training in place, you can still educate yourself – personally, I love using Google Alerts to find out what's happening in the world at the moment. Staff should request formal awareness training from their line managers. Your company might also prepare for attacks by carrying out frequent cyber crisis simulation exercises to prepare their response to a cyberattack using phishing simulation emails, for example.

Follow your company IT policy, and don't break the rules! You should always store documents on corporate structures, use the VPN, and do not use personal devices to access company data and emails. Never, by any means, allow your family members or friends to use your company-owned devices. Using your company VPN when you are accessing the company network will help you stay secure, especially when you are connecting to public Wi-Fi.

All WFH employees could also implement home internet protection and monitoring. There are loads of tools available to protect your home's internet with just a few simple and basic changes to your router, and some are free! This will stop potentially dangerous ransomware and prevent access to malicious websites from personal, family, and company devices.

And let's not forget updates – never ever! Always ensure you have all home devices updated with the latest security patches and have the best anti-virus and anti-malware software installed. This will prevent potential internal home network hijacks. Your regular updates should also include mobile phone devices and network routers. Don't connect unknown or random devices to your company-owned or personal devices.

Create a home IT policy to help and educate your family or housemates. You should agree to always follow fixed rules. For example, don't download or install illegal software or movies, which can lead to a home network slowdown, exploitation, and potentially great financial liability. Part of your home IT strategy should always have a built-in password policy. Change and enable passwords and ensure all devices have strong, unique passwords to prevent any unauthorized access. Whatever you do, don't use your home internet router's default password for your Wi-Fi or to access the router. Always ensure you lock your company-owned devices when you are away from your workspace. With the increasing popularity of IoT, make sure that these devices are updated and secure. Tsedal Neeley, a professor at Harvard Business School, says this is what

SME managers should do to get the best out of their employees when they WFH:

> "Get the infrastructure right. Do people have the requisite technology or access to it? Who has a laptop? Will those who do [have laptops] be able to dial in to their organizations easily? Will they have the software they need to be able to do work, have conference calls, and so forth? What about the employees who don't have laptops or mobile devices? How do you make sure that they have access to the resources they need to do work? Direct managers have to very quickly ensure that every employee has full access so that no one feels left behind."[18]

As part of a home IT policy, all employees should be warned about the dangers of digital piracy or illegally downloading software, music or movies. It's totally illegal, breaking copyright and intellectual property (IP) laws, and can land anyone in hot water with hefty fines and even prison time. In the UK, depending on what you are found to be guilty of, the sentence when convicted of breaking a digital piracy copyright law can be as much as five years imprisonment with a £5,000 fine. However, the hazards associated with digital piracy extend beyond legal consequences. Malware and vulnerabilities introduced through pirated content pose significant risks to systems, making them susceptible to common forms of cyberattack.

And now another one of my favourites - backups. Remember that backup is king. Always ensure you have at least one backup for photos and files on your personal devices - or two! Never assume that if you are using a cloud storage system, it automatically backs up your data. It goes without saying that data backups are undeniably critical. Lost data can easily have a massive impact on your productivity, your customer's experience and opinion of your company, business operations, and revenue. Former CISO at Cisco, Hylton Stewart, says:

> "The main thing that makes data backup important is disaster recovery and business continuity. From a deleted business file to a company-wide ransomware infection that encrypts all files, having a data backup solution in place and managed allows for the faster recovery of information and assets. It enables you to restore deleted files and rebuild critical servers in a fraction of the time it would take to start from scratch."[19]

Stewart also highlights the extent of human error in security breaches, and says:

> "More than 40% of reported security breaches are caused by employee negligence."[20]

That we know, and it's not going to change. I've said in other chapters that we can't continue to blame people and human error. More training will help, but security awareness, sticking to the basics, and a cultural change are what will really make the difference between getting breached and not.

Going back to backup basics for a minute. Online storage and backup that allows you to store photos, videos, and files - accessible through the web or app - is owned by someone else: the provider. There are a few known and trusted providers that offer some storage at no charge or for a minimal fee. These include Google Drive, Apple iCloud, OneDrive, and Amazon Drive. If you are an Amazon Prime member, you get unlimited photo storage space. How much storage do I need? The more files you have, the more storage you need. A good guide for storage requirements is that 2 GB gives you enough space for 1,000 images, 20,000 documents, or five minutes of HD video. Don't use personal cloud storage for business data.

And now some tips to keep your personal data safe in cloud storage. Change your password regularly, and don't use predictable passwords. Whenever possible, use MFA. When it comes to sensitive files, always double check where you are storing them and backing them up to. For example, using a family account means that others might have access to the files. Possibly use another device for sensitive data and make sure you keep your devices updated and PIN protected.

We discussed phishing scams during the pandemic earlier. These continue, now more than ever. Criminals are devious opportunists who will use fearmongering related to local or global disasters to take advantage of people. As they did in the COVID-19 pandemic, they continue to prey on all and sundry. But do not fret and allow these threats to overwhelm you and lure you into making mistakes. Some commonly known scams you need to look out for, and ones that were common during the pandemic, include fake websites, the sale of bogus medical equipment, deceptive miracle cures, vaccines and treatments, expedited stimulus checks, fake small business loans, and donation scams. These bad actors often use social media channels to get you to engage and will, from time to time, claim to be local government officials. In 2020, the Federal Trade Commission reported:

> "Coronavirus-related scams have cost Americans $13.4 million so far this year."[21]

Phishing scams may be unsophisticated and annoying, but their frequency makes them a matter of concern. Phishing emails are the most common attack used by cybercriminals, and the risks and opportunities increase when working remotely. Always be on the lookout for emails from a suspicious sender and with strange and unexpected attachments from known and unknown senders. Emails requesting confirmation of personal and financial information are definitely dodgy. Requests to *click here* even if it looks like it is from a legitimate sender or vendor, must be avoided. The same applies to requests to change your password, but first, to confirm your credentials. Language structure and tone can also give us clues that something is not right. Poor grammar and spelling mistakes imply that the sender doesn't have English as a mother tongue. Aggressive, demanding, and threatening language, or that trying to make you panic, is also often a giveaway. Unfortunately, with the likes of ChatGPT in our midst, foreign hackers can easily overcome language barriers as you saw when we discussed online fraud.

The reality is that cyberattacks will continue to grow, and SMEs will have to look at radically strengthening their cyber defenses around their critical infrastructure. However, implementing all the controls and measures that I've spoken about will go a long way to helping businesses and keep their remote workforce safe. I'll leave you now with these words:

> "You don't need a £1 million cybersecurity budget. You just need common sense and to apply the basics. Always. End of story."

About the Author

Izak Oosthuizen – Chief Executive Officer of Zhero Limited, cybersecurity expert, best-selling author, and London EO Member.

Izak is a London IT thought leader, entrepreneur, and cybersecurity expert. He is a member of the Entrepreneur's Organisation London and was nominated for the prestigious UKTech50 award in 2022.

In 2006, Izak founded Zhero, a London-headquartered end-to-end business cybersecurity and IT support company for SMEs. Zhero is a Microsoft Gold partner providing tailored risk mitigation, cybersecurity, cloud, IT support, consultancy, and professional services to many industry sectors, including medical, finance, legal, insurance, and architecture. Zhero has worked with a diverse range of clients and institutions such as WeWork, Giorgio Armani, Energy UK, Edmond De Rothschild, the Federation of Master Builders, City, University of London and Dimension Data.

Izak is the co-author of two best-selling IT books, 'Adapt and Overcome' and 'Cybersecurity NOW', both available on Amazon. These are essential reads for navigating the ever-changing worlds of cybersecurity, remote working, and the digitised workplace. His insights have also been featured in The Economist, UK Computer Weekly and other prominent publications.

Izak is a respected keynote speaker and has participated in events hosted by The Economist, N-Able, London Market Forums (LMF), and others. At the recent LMF 2023 Cyber Resilience Leaders' Summit, he shared cutting-edge cybersecurity and risk mitigation strategies with contemporary pioneers such as Gary Brailsford-Hart, the Director of Information & CISO at City of London Police, and Simon Newman, the CEO of the Cyber Resilience Centre for London.

Izak holds several IT qualifications – including various Microsoft, Checkpoint and VMware certifications. Combined with his 20-plus years of experience in IT, and management qualifications from the London School of Business & Finance and Cranfield School of Management, he appreciates that IT drives growth but also comes with associated security risks.

As an individual, Izak is determined and likes to get the job done. His sense of humour makes him an accomplished 'connector' and his humble past allows others to relate to him with a personal touch. Izak's ability to simplify life's complexities instils trust and inspires those around him, both professionally and personally. Izak is an avid proponent of the Biblical philosophy described in Proverbs 11:24: "The world of the generous gets larger and larger…"

Besides being a Christian, much of Izak's inspiration comes from Chuck Feeney, the American businessman and philanthropist, known as the "James Bond of Philanthropy." Chuck was 'The Billionaire Who Wanted to Die Broke,' and believed in the joy of giving while living. At the age of 89, he achieved his lifelong goal of giving away all of his amassed fortune – the sum of $8 billion! Inspired by Chuck's generosity, Izak continues to build a company with a Christian ethos and a strong sense of purpose. He aims to bring hope and also play a part in breaking the cycle of poverty. Above all, Izak has faith in the Christian message that he believes has the power to change any generation.

Believing that it has power to set people free, regardless heartbreaking cycles we often see in families or generations and that we are called to freedom, a life in abundance until it overflows, above and beyond what we can ask, think, or imagine. Something he has experienced himself.

References

Chapter 1

[1] Freshworks - Top IT Quotes: https://www.freshworks.com/freshservice/general/top-it-quotes-blog/

[2] Independent Advisor 31 May 2023 - 15 cybercrime statistics you ought to know: https://www.independent.co.uk/advisor/vpn/cybercrime-statistics

[3] Cisco Press Release 18 February 2020 - New Cisco Annual Internet Report Forecasts 5G to Support More Than 10% of Global Mobile Connections by 2023: https://newsroom.cisco.com/c/r/newsroom/en/us/a/y2020/m02/new-cisco-annual-internet-report-forecasts-5g-to-support-more-than-10-of-global-mobile-connections-by-2023.html

[4] Rapid Scale - Cybercrime: The Greatest Threat to Business Today: https://rapidscale.net/resources/blog/managed-cloud-services/cybercrime-the-greatest-threat-to-business-today

[5] Astra 2 August 2023 - 30+ Malware Statistics You Need To Know In 2023: https://www.getastra.com/blog/security-audit/malware-statistics/

[6] AV-Test – Malware: https://www.av-test.org/en/statistics/malware/

[7] Astra 2 August 2023 - 30+ Malware Statistics You Need To Know In 2023: https://www.getastra.com/blog/security-audit/malware-statistics/

---

[8] Digital Guardian 28 December 2022 - A History of Ransomware Attacks: The Biggest and Worst Ransomware Attacks of All Time: https://www.digitalguardian.com/blog/history-ransomware-attacks-biggest-and-worst-ransomware-attacks-all-time

[9] The Guardian17 July 2023 - Who are the ransomware gangs wreaking havoc on the world's biggest companies: https://www.theguardian.com/commentisfree/2023/jul/17/ransomware-gangs-companies-cyber-crime-hackers

[10] Wikipedia – WannaCry ransomware attack: https://en.wikipedia.org/wiki/WannaCry_ransomware_attack

[11] Simplilearn 1 August 2023 - SolarWinds Attack And All The Details You Need To Know About It: https://www.simplilearn.com/tutorials/cryptography-tutorial/all-about-solarwinds-attack

[12] Wikipedia - JBS S.A. ransomware attack: https://en.wikipedia.org/wiki/JBS_S.A._ransomware_attack

[13] Astra 4 August 2023 - 100+ Ransomware Attack Statistics 2023: Trends & Cost: https://www.getastra.com/blog/security-audit/ransomware-attack-statistics/

[14] ICO 8 July 2022 - ICO and NCSC stand together against ransomware payments being made: https://ico.org.uk/about-the-ico/media-centre/news-and-blogs/2022/07/ico-and-ncsc-stand-together-against-ransomware-payments-being-made/

[15] ICO 8 July 2022 - ICO and NCSC stand together against ransomware payments being made: https://ico.org.uk/about-the-

ico/media-centre/news-and-blogs/2022/07/ico-and-ncsc-stand-together-against-ransomware-payments-being-made/

[16] PC Mag UK 30 September 2022 - Wrong Numbers, Fake Invoices, and Catfishing: How to Avoid the Top Internet Scams: https://uk.pcmag.com/security/142985/wrong-numbers-fake-invoices-and-catfishing-how-to-spot-and-avoid-the-top-internet-scams

[17] AAG 2 October 2023 - The Latest 2023 Phishing Statistics: https://aag-it.com/the-latest-phishing-statistics/

[18] The Cloudflare Blog 16 August 2023 - Introducing Cloudflare's 2023 phishing threats report: https://blog.cloudflare.com/2023-phishing-report/

[19] CNET 25 February 2004 - Gates predicts death of the password: https://www.cnet.com/news/privacy/gates-predicts-death-of-the-password/

[20] Becker's Health IT 14 June 2023 - 30 most common passwords of 2023: https://www.beckershospitalreview.com/cybersecurity/30-most-common-passwords-of-2023.html

[21] Solutions Review 31 March 2023 - 45 World Backup Day Quotes from 32 Experts for 2023: https://solutionsreview.com/backup-disaster-recovery/world-backup-day-quotes/

[22] IBM Annual Report 2013 – What will we make of this moment: https://www.ibm.com/annualreport/2013/bin/assets/2013_ibm_annual.pdf

[23] Solutions Review 31 March 2023 - 45 World Backup Day Quotes from 32 Experts for 2023: https://solutionsreview.com/backup-disaster-recovery/world-backup-day-quotes/

[24] Native Intelligence 25 March 2020 – Security Quotes: https://www.nativeintelligence.com/resources/security-quotes/

Chapter 2

[1] Pinngle 31 August 2019 - 99 Inspiring Cybersecurity Quotes: https://pinngle.me/blog/99-inspiring-cybersecurity-quotes/

[2] GOV.UK Cyber Security Breaches Survey 2022 11 July 2022: https://www.gov.uk/government/statistics/cyber-security-breaches-survey-2022/cyber-security-breaches-survey-2022

[3] GOV.UK Cyber Security Breaches Survey 2022 11 July 2022: https://www.gov.uk/government/statistics/cyber-security-breaches-survey-2022/cyber-security-breaches-survey-2022

[4] Solutions Review 31 March 2023 - 45 World Backup Day Quotes from 32 Experts for 2023: https://solutionsreview.com/backup-disaster-recovery/world-backup-day-quotes/

[5] Native Intelligence 25 March 2020 – Security Quotes: https://www.nativeintelligence.com/resources/security-quotes/

[6] ITPro 30 March 2022 - NCSC warns businesses against using Kaspersky products: https://www.itpro.com/security/antivirus/367251/ncsc-kaspersky-warning

[7] NIST Taking Measure 28 October 2020 - Zero Trust Cybersecurity: 'Never Trust, Always Verify': https://www.nist.gov/blogs/taking-measure/zero-trust-cybersecurity-never-trust-always-verify

[8] Forbes 26 April 2021 - Update Your Mac Now: The 'Worst Hack In Years' Hits Apple Computers: https://www.forbes.com/sites/thomasbrewster/2021/04/26/update-your-mac-now-the-worst-hack-in-years-hits-apple-computers/?sh=1e3256fc5da0

[9] Security 21 June 2023 - 3 in 4 people at risk of being hacked due to poor password practices: https://www.securitymagazine.com/articles/99529-3-in-4-people-at-risk-of-being-hacked-due-to-poor-password-practices

[10] Native Intelligence 25 March 2020 – Security Quotes: https://www.nativeintelligence.com/resources/security-quotes/

[11] Astra 4 August 2023 - 81 Phishing Attack Statistics 2023: The Ultimate Insight: https://www.getastra.com/blog/security-audit/phishing-attack-statistics/

[12] Native Intelligence 25 March 2020 – Security Quotes: https://www.nativeintelligence.com/resources/security-quotes/

[13] Native Intelligence 25 March 2020 – Security Quotes: https://www.nativeintelligence.com/resources/security-quotes/

[14] Reuters 3 August 2021 - Kaseya ransomware attack sets off race to hack service providers -researchers: https://www.reuters.com/technology/kaseya-ransomware-attack-sets-off-race-hack-service-providers-researchers-2021-08-03/

[15] Reuters 3 August 2021 - Kaseya ransomware attack sets off race to hack service providers -researchers: https://www.reuters.com/technology/kaseya-ransomware-attack-sets-off-race-hack-service-providers-researchers-2021-08-03/

[16] Native Intelligence 25 March 2020 – Security Quotes: https://www.nativeintelligence.com/resources/security-quotes/

Chapter 3

[1] Cybersophia - Hacker and Hacking Quotes & Sayings: https://cybersophia.net/quotes/hacker-and-hacking-quotes-sayings/

[2] Wikipedia – Window Snyder: https://en.wikipedia.org/wiki/Window_Snyder

[3] GOV.UK - Cyber security breaches survey 2023: https://www.gov.uk/government/statistics/cyber-security-breaches-survey-2023/cyber-security-breaches-survey-2023

[4] Independent Advisor 31 May 2023 - 15 cybercrime statistics you ought to know: https://www.independent.co.uk/advisor/vpn/cybercrime-statistics

[5] AAG 2 August 2023 - The Latest 2023 Ransomware Statistics (updated August 2023): https://aag-it.com/the-latest-ransomware-statistics/

[6] Computer Weekly 3 August 2016 - One in five businesses hit by ransomware are forced to close, study shows: https://www.computerweekly.com/news/450301845/One-in-five-businesses-hit-by-ransomware-are-forced-to-close-study-shows

[7] AAG 2 August 2023 - The Latest 2023 Ransomware Statistics (updated August 2023): https://aag-it.com/the-latest-ransomware-statistics/

[8] Huntsman 10 April 2018 - Cyber Security Quotes: 5 useful quotes from organisations that have been hacked: https://huntsmansecurity.com/blog/5-useful-quotes-from-hacked-organisations/

[9] The Register 23 August 2023 - Criminals go full Viking on CloudNordic, wipe all servers and customer data: https://www.theregister.com/AMP/2023/08/23/ransomware_wipes_cloudnordic/

[10] Financial Times 11 September 2023 - Ransomware thrives as cyber security remains lax, says UK report: https://www.ft.com/content/0d1d3b49-4eb9-42b4-89b3-e4c828014ccd

[11] Ransomware, extortion and the cybercrime ecosystem - A white paper from the NCSC and the NCA: https://www.ncsc.gov.uk/files/White-paper-Ransomware-extortion-and-the-cyber-crime-ecosystem.pdf

[12] Ransomware, extortion and the cybercrime ecosystem - A white paper from the NCSC and the NCA: https://www.ncsc.gov.uk/files/White-paper-Ransomware-extortion-and-the-cyber-crime-ecosystem.pdf

[13] Ransomware, extortion and the cybercrime ecosystem - A white paper from the NCSC and the NCA: https://www.ncsc.gov.uk/files/White-paper-Ransomware-extortion-and-the-cyber-crime-ecosystem.pdf

---

[14] Sky News 14 September 2023 - MGM Resorts cyberattack: Casinos warned to be on 'high alert' as £11bn firm remains crippled: https://news.sky.com/story/mgm-resorts-cyberattack-casinos-warned-to-be-on-high-alert-as-11bn-firm-remains-crippled-12960944

[15] Las Vegas Review Journal 17 September 2023 - Analyst: MGM losing $4.2M-$8.4M a day because of cyberattack: https://www.reviewjournal.com/business/casinos-gaming/analyst-mgm-losing-4-2m-8-4m-a-day-because-of-cyberattack-2906379/

[16] Nevada Independent 19 September 2023 - MGM's losses in cyberattack will be insured up to $200 million: https://thenevadaindependent.com/article/mgms-losses-in-cyberattack-will-be-insured-up-to-200-million

[17] CNBC 14 September 2023 - Caesars paid millions in ransom to cybercrime group prior to MGM hack: https://www.cnbc.com/2023/09/14/caesars-paid-millions-in-ransom-to-cybercrime-group-prior-to-mgm-hack.html

[18] CSO 8 November 2022 - The 15 biggest data breaches of the 21st century: https://www.csoonline.com/article/534628/the-biggest-data-breaches-of-the-21st-century.html

[19] Brainy Quote – Hackers Quotes: https://www.brainyquote.com/topics/hackers-quotes

[20] Cybersophia - Hacker and Hacking Quotes & Sayings: https://cybersophia.net/quotes/hacker-and-hacking-quotes-sayings/

[21] Deloitte – Cyber Simulation-in-a-box: https://www2.deloitte.com/content/dam/Deloitte/cy/Documents/risk/crs/CY_Risk_CyberSimulationInABoxFlyer_Noexp.pdf

[22] KnowBe4 - Stanford Research: 88% Of Data Breaches Are Caused By Human Error: https://blog.knowbe4.com/88-percent-of-data-breaches-are-caused-by-human-error

[23] Comparitech 13 June 2023 - 30+ data breach statistics and facts: https://www.comparitech.com/blog/vpn-privacy/data-breach-statistics-facts/

[24] PK Tech 13 March 2021 - Report Finds Companies Have Massive Amounts of Inactive User Accounts: https://www.pktech.net/2021/03/report-finds-companies-have-massive-amounts-of-inactive-user-accounts/

[25] 2018 Varonis Global Data Risk Report: https://info.varonis.com/hubfs/2018%20Varonis%20Global%20Data%20Risk%20Report.pdf

[26] Solutions Review - 45 World Backup Day Quotes from 32 Experts for 2023: https://solutionsreview.com/backup-disaster-recovery/world-backup-day-quotes/

[27] AZ Quotes – Password Quotes: https://www.azquotes.com/quotes/topics/passwords.html

Chapter 4

[1] World Economic Forum Cybersecurity 3 March 2023 - 7 trends that could shape the future of cybersecurity in 2030: https://www.weforum.org/agenda/2023/03/trends-for-future-of-cybersecurity/

[2] Veritis Transcend - Global Cloud Market to Reach Nearly USD 800 Billion by 2028: Survey: https://www.veritis.com/news/global-cloud-market-to-reach-nearly-usd-800-billion-by-2028-survey/

[3] Trapp Technology 15 May 2013 - 10 Must-Read Quotes about Cloud Computing: https://trapptechnology.com/10-must-read-quotes-about-cloud-computing/

[4] Veritis Transcend - All You Need to Know About Top 10 Security Issues in Cloud Computing: https://www.veritis.com/blog/top-10-security-issues-in-cloud-computing/

[5] University of Salford Manchester - CYBERSECURITY ISN'T A PRIORITY FOR SMES, RIGHT? CHANGE YOUR STRATEGY!: https://www.salford.ac.uk/working-with-business/greater-manchester-cyber-foundry/cybersecurity-isnt-a-priority-for-smes-right

[6] Mane 22 February 2023 - Cyberattacks on the Rise for SME UK businesses: Why you should care: https://www.mane.co.uk/news/cyber-attacks-on-the-rise-for-sme-uk-businesses-why-you-should-care-299715/

[7] Leyton 10 January 2023 - UK Small and Medium-Sized Enterprises (SMEs) Statistics: https://leyton.com/uk/insights/articles/uk-sme-statistics

[8] Netwrix 4 August 2023 - The Importance of Security Risk Assessments and How to Conduct Them: https://blog.netwrix.com/2023/08/04/it-risk-assessment/

[9] [9] OECD iLibrary - Artificial intelligence: Changing landscape for SMEs: https://www.oecd-ilibrary.org/sites/01a4ae9d-en/index.html?itemId=/content/component/01a4ae9d-en

[10] World Economic Forum 22 July 2022 - IoT can help small and medium businesses implement sustainability measures. Here's how: https://www.weforum.org/agenda/2022/07/iot-small-medium-businesses-profitable-sustainable/

Chapter 5

[1] Forbes 12 September 2018 - 19 Astonishing Quotes About The Internet Of Things Everyone Should Read: https://www.forbes.com/sites/bernardmarr/2018/09/12/19-astonishing-quotes-about-the-internet-of-things-everyone-should-read/

[2] Fortune Business Insights April 2023 - The Internet of Things (IoT) Market: https://www.fortunebusinessinsights.com/industry-reports/internet-of-things-iot-market-100307

[3] Statista - Number of Internet of Things (IoT) connected devices worldwide from 2019 to 2023, with forecasts from 2022 to 2030: https://www.statista.com/statistics/1183457/iot-connected-devices-worldwide/

[4] Semiconductor Digest - Number of connected IoT devices will surge to 125 billion by 2030: https://sst.semiconductor-digest.com/2017/10/number-of-connected-iot-devices-will-surge-to-125-billion-by-2030/

[5] IoT, an explosion of connected possibilities and vulnerabilities, Jose Monteagudo: https://cyberstartupobservatory.com/iot-explosion-connected-possibilities/

[6] CBI Ministry Of Foreign Affairs Netherlands 7 June 2022 - The European market potential for (Industrial) Internet of Things:

https://www.cbi.eu/market-information/outsourcing-itobpo/industrial-internet-things/market-potential

[7] BT 2 November 2021 – What does the Internet of Things (IoT) mean for small businesses: https://business.bt.com/why-choose-bt/insights/internet-of-things/what-is-the-internet-of-things-for-small-and-medium-businesses/

[8] BT 2 November 2021 – What does the Internet of Things (IoT) mean for small businesses: https://business.bt.com/why-choose-bt/insights/internet-of-things/what-is-the-internet-of-things-for-small-and-medium-businesses/

[9] World Economic Forum 22 July 2022 - IoT can help small and medium businesses implement sustainability measures. Here's how: https://www.weforum.org/agenda/2022/07/iot-small-medium-businesses-profitable-sustainable/

[10] Pew Research Centre 6 June 2017 - Theme 1: People crave connection and convenience, and a tech-linked world serves both goals well: https://www.pewresearch.org/internet/2017/06/06/theme-1-people-crave-connection-and-convenience-and-a-tech-linked-world-serves-both-goals-well/

[11] Picus Security 14 September 2022 - UK Finance sector reports increase in DDoS-related cyber incidents: https://www.picussecurity.com/resource/fca-data-reveals-increase-in-ddos-incidents

[12] The Guardian 23 January 2017 - Lloyds bank accounts targeted in huge cybercrime attack: https://www.theguardian.com/business/2017/jan/23/lloyds-bank-accounts-targeted-cybercrime-attack

[13] Cyber Management Alliance 25 October 2022 - IoT Security: 5 cyber-attacks caused by IoT security vulnerabilities: https://www.cm-alliance.com/cybersecurity-blog/iot-security-5-cyber-attacks-caused-by-iot-security-vulnerabilities

[14] Good Reads – IoT Quotes: https://www.goodreads.com/quotes/tag/iot

[15] Cloudflare 14 December 2017 - Inside the infamous Mirai IoT Botnet: A Retrospective Analysis: https://blog.cloudflare.com/inside-mirai-the-infamous-iot-botnet-a-retrospective-analysis/

[16] The Register 5 September 2019 - Newb admits he ran Satori botnet that turned thousands of hacked devices into a 100Gbps+ DDoS-for-hire cannon: https://www.theregister.com/2019/09/05/satori_plea_deal/

[17] Inmarsat 15 March 2022 - Skills shortages remain the top barrier to industrial IoT adoption, Inmarsat research reveals: https://www.inmarsat.com/en/news/latest-news/enterprise/2022/skills-shortage-iot-adoption-research.html

[18] f5 labs 5 August 2019 - The Hunt for IoT: So Easy To Compromise, Children Are Doing It: https://www.f5.com/labs/articles/threat-intelligence/the-hunt-for-iot--so-easy-to-compromise--children-are-doing-it

Chapter 6

[1] Analytics India Magazine 29 February 2020 - Top Ten Best Quotes By Elon Musk On AI: https://analyticsindiamag.com/top-ten-best-quotes-by-elon-musk-on-artificial-intelligence/

[2] Forbes 12 September 2018 - 19 Astonishing Quotes About The Internet Of Things Everyone Should Read: https://www.forbes.com/sites/bernardmarr/2018/09/12/19-astonishing-quotes-about-the-internet-of-things-everyone-should-read

[3] Forbes Advisor 26 June 2023 - UK Artificial Intelligence (AI) Statistics And Trends In 2023: https://www.forbes.com/uk/advisor/business/software/uk-artificial-intelligence-ai-statistics-2023/

[4] Forbes Advisor 26 June 2023 - UK Artificial Intelligence (AI) Statistics And Trends In 2023: https://www.forbes.com/uk/advisor/business/software/uk-artificial-intelligence-ai-statistics-2023/

[5] BBC Science Focus - ChatGPT: Everything you need to know about OpenAI's GPT-4 tool: https://www.sciencefocus.com/future-technology/gpt-3

[6] OECD Library Artificial intelligence: Changing landscape for SMEs: https://www.oecd-ilibrary.org/sites/01a4ae9d-en/index.html?itemId=/content/component/01a4ae9d-en

[7] Grand View Research - Artificial Intelligence Market Size, Share & Trends Analysis Report By Solution, By Technology (Deep Learning, Machine Learning), By End-use, By Region, And Segment Forecasts, 2023 – 2030: https://www.grandviewresearch.com/industry-analysis/artificial-intelligence-ai-market

[8] Info Security Magazine 18 January 2023 - ChatGPT Creates Polymorphic Malware: https://www.infosecurity-magazine.com/news/chatgpt-creates-polymorphic-malware/

[9] Info Security Magazine 15 March 2023 - Will ChatGPT Democratize the Development of Evasive Malware: https://www.infosecurity-magazine.com/blogs/chatgpt-democratize-evasive-malware/

[10] Info Security Magazine 15 March 2023 - Will ChatGPT Democratize the Development of Evasive Malware: https://www.infosecurity-magazine.com/blogs/chatgpt-democratize-evasive-malware/

[11] Forbes 8 September 2022 - Deepfakes - The Danger Of Artificial Intelligence That We Will Learn To Manage Better: https://www.forbes.com/sites/lutzfinger/2022/09/08/deepfakesthe-danger-of-artificial-intelligence-that-we-will-learn-to-manage-better/

[12] Evening Standard - AI-generated content appears in LinkedIn phishing scams, but can users spot it: https://www.standard.co.uk/tech/ai-content-used-linkedin-phishing-scams-users-spot-it-b1062721.html

[13] Investor Place 17 May 2023 - What Does Elon Musk Really Think About AI? 3 Revealing Quotes From His CNBC Interview: https://investorplace.com/2023/05/what-does-elon-musk-really-think-about-ai-3-revealing-quotes-from-his-cnbc-interview/

[14] Investor Place 17 May 2023 - What Does Elon Musk Really Think About AI? 3 Revealing Quotes From His CNBC Interview: https://investorplace.com/2023/05/what-does-elon-musk-really-think-about-ai-3-revealing-quotes-from-his-cnbc-interview/

Chapter 7

[1] Comply GDPR - How GDPR affects your business: https://www.complygdpr.com/about-gdpr/

[2] GOV.UK Press release - Cyber security boost for UK firms: https://www.gov.uk/government/news/cyber-security-boost-for-uk-firms

Chapter 8

[1] CSO 7 February 2023 - 7 reasons to avoid investing in cyber insurance: https://www.csoonline.com/article/574591/7-reasons-to-avoid-investing-in-cyber-insurance.html

[2] Munich RE Global Cyber Risk and Insurance Survey 2022: https://www.munichre.com/landingpage/en/global-cyber-risk-and-insurance-survey-2022.html

[3] Insurance Times 10 October 2022 - Cyber insurance uptake with SMEs remains low – GlobalData: https://www.insurancetimes.co.uk/news/cyber-insurance-uptake-with-smes-remains-low-globaldata/

[4] CSO 7 February 2023 - 7 reasons to avoid investing in cyber insurance: https://www.csoonline.com/article/574591/7-reasons-to-avoid-investing-in-cyber-insurance.html

[5] CSO 7 February 2023 - 7 reasons to avoid investing in cyber insurance: https://www.csoonline.com/article/574591/7-reasons-to-avoid-investing-in-cyber-insurance.html

[6] Tech Target - Ransomware trends, statistics and facts in 2023: https://www.techtarget.com/searchsecurity/feature/Ransomware-trends-statistics-and-facts

[7] Tech Monitor 30 6 October 2022 - Is the cyber insurance market broken?: https://techmonitor.ai/technology/cybersecurity/is-the-cyber-insurance-market-broken

Chapter 9

[1] Brainy Quote – Fraud Quotes: https://www.brainyquote.com/quotes/maria_konnikova_1110720?src=t_fraud

[2] BBC 5 May 2023 - Banks warn of big increase in online scams: https://www.bbc.co.uk/news/technology-65486219

[3] This is Money 23 August 2023 - I fell victim to a Facebook scam and the police advised me to write a letter of complaint to Mark Zuckerberg: https://www.thisismoney.co.uk/money/beatthescammers/article-12434297/Are-police-powerless-tackle-fraud-Facebook-victims-better-complaining-Mark-Zuckerberg.html

[4] BBC 5 May 2023 - Banks warn of big increase in online scams: https://www.bbc.co.uk/news/technology-65486219

[5] BBC 5 May 2023 - Banks warn of big increase in online scams: https://www.bbc.co.uk/news/technology-65486219

[6] BBC 5 May 2023 - Banks warn of big increase in online scams: https://www.bbc.co.uk/news/technology-65486219

[7] NCA – Fraud: https://www.nationalcrimeagency.gov.uk/what-we-do/crime-threats/fraud-and-economic-crime

[8] UK Finance - OVER £1.2 BILLION STOLEN THROUGH FRAUD IN 2022, WITH NEARLY 80 PER CENT OF APP FRAUD CASES STARTING ONLINE: https://www.ukfinance.org.uk/news-and-insight/press-release/over-ps12-billion-stolen-through-fraud-in-2022-nearly-80-cent-app

[9] UK Finance - OVER £1.2 BILLION STOLEN THROUGH FRAUD IN 2022, WITH NEARLY 80 PER CENT OF APP FRAUD CASES STARTING ONLINE: https://www.ukfinance.org.uk/news-and-insight/press-release/over-ps12-billion-stolen-through-fraud-in-2022-nearly-80-cent-app

[10] UK Finance - OVER £1.2 BILLION STOLEN THROUGH FRAUD IN 2022, WITH NEARLY 80 PER CENT OF APP FRAUD CASES STARTING ONLINE: https://www.ukfinance.org.uk/news-and-insight/press-release/over-ps12-billion-stolen-through-fraud-in-2022-nearly-80-cent-app

[11] Metropolitan Police – Cybercrime: https://www.met.police.uk/advice/advice-and-information/fa/fraud/online-fraud/cyber-crime-fraud/

[12] Ofcom 16 March 2023 - Scale and impact of online fraud revealed: https://www.ofcom.org.uk/news-centre/2023/scale-and-impact-of-online-fraud-revealed

[13] Ofcom 16 March 2023 - Scale and impact of online fraud revealed: https://www.ofcom.org.uk/news-centre/2023/scale-and-impact-of-online-fraud-revealed

[14] Ofcom 16 March 2023 - Scale and impact of online fraud revealed: https://www.ofcom.org.uk/news-centre/2023/scale-and-impact-of-online-fraud-revealed

[15] GAVC LAW – GEERT VAN CALSTER – 7 June 2019 The internet's not written in pencil, it's written in ink. Szpunar AG in Eva Glawischnig-Piesczek v Facebook, re i.a. jurisdiction and removal of hate speech. (As well as confirming my reading of his Opinion in Google): https://gavclaw.com/2019/06/07/the-internets-not-written-in-pencil-its-written-in-ink-szpunar-ag-in-eva-glawischnig-piesczek-v-facebook-re-i-a-jurisdiction-and-removal-of-hate-speech-as-well-as-confirming-my/

[16] PC Mag UK 30 September 2022 - Wrong Numbers, Fake Invoices, and Catfishing: How to Avoid the Top Internet Scams: https://uk.pcmag.com/security/142985/wrong-numbers-fake-invoices-and-catfishing-how-to-spot-and-avoid-the-top-internet-scams

[17] PC Mag UK 30 September 2022 - Wrong Numbers, Fake Invoices, and Catfishing: How to Avoid the Top Internet Scams: https://uk.pcmag.com/security/142985/wrong-numbers-fake-invoices-and-catfishing-how-to-spot-and-avoid-the-top-internet-scams

[18] PC Mag UK 5 Match 2021 - FTC Shuts Down Massive Robocall Charity Scam: https://uk.pcmag.com/security/132101/ftc-shuts-down-massive-robocall-charity-scam

[19] UNITED STATES DISTRICT COURT EASTERN DISTRICT OF MICHIGAN SOUTHERN DIVISION - Case 2:21-cv-10174-DML-CI: https://www.ftc.gov/system/files/documents/cases/1_-_complaint_2.pdf

Chapter 10

[1] Cyber Resilience Insights 15 February 2022 - Why Is Cybersecurity Important in the Post-Pandemic World: https://www.mimecast.com/blog/why-is-cybersecurity-important-in-the-post-pandemic-world/

[2] Office for National Statistics 8 July 2020 - Coronavirus and homeworking in the UK: April 2020: https://www.ons.gov.uk/employmentandlabourmarket/peopleinwork/employmentandemployeetypes/bulletins/coronavirusandhomeworkingintheuk/april2020

[3] Statista - Percentage of adults that have worked from home or travelled to work at some point in the previous seven days in Great Britain(March 2020 to May 2023): https://www.statista.com/statistics/1207746/coronavirus-working-location-trends-britain/

[4] swissinfo.ch 7 June 2020 - Jump in cyberattacks during Covid-19 confinement: https://www.swissinfo.ch/eng/jump-in-cyber-attacks-during-covid-19-confinement/45818794

[5] Deloitte - Impact of COVID-19 on Cybersecurity: https://www2.deloitte.com/ch/en/pages/risk/articles/impact-covid-cybersecurity.html

[6] Tessian 7 September 2020 - Why We Click: The Psychology Behind Phishing Scams and How to Avoid Being Hacked: https://www.tessian.com/blog/why-we-click-on-phishing-scams/

[7] Databasix - Statistics Of Cyber Security Risks When Working from Home: https://www.dbxuk.com/statistics/cyber-security-risks-wfh

[8] Tessian 7 September 2020 - Why We Click: The Psychology Behind Phishing Scams and How to Avoid Being Hacked: https://www.tessian.com/blog/why-we-click-on-phishing-scams/

[9] CPO Magazine 8 June 2020 - Google-Branded Phishing Attacks Account for 65% of Threats Facing Remote Workers: https://www.cpomagazine.com/cyber-security/google-branded-phishing-attacks-account-for-65-of-threats-facing-remote-workers/

[10] Fox News 25 April 2020 - 10 COVID-19 scams spreading right now that people are falling for: https://www.foxnews.com/tech/10-covid-19-scams-spreading-right-now-that-people-are-falling-for

[11] Cynet - Covid19 Cyberattack Analysis: https://go.cynet.com/covid-19-cyberattack-analysis?utm_source=thn

[12] National Fraud and Cyber Crime Reporting Centre - COVID-19 related scams - news and resources: https://www.actionfraud.police.uk/covid19

[13] Biz Community 15 May 2020 - Keep VPNs safe from DDoS and other attacks as remote working continues: https://www.bizcommunity.com/Article/196/661/203954.html

[14] Check Point 12 May 2020 - Coronavirus cyber-attacks update: beware of the phish: https://blog.checkpoint.com/security/coronavirus-cyber-attacks-update-beware-of-the-phish/

[15] Tampa Bay Times 12 June 2020 - Pasco PTA Zoom meeting gets hacked with porn, racist rants: https://www.tampabay.com/news/pasco/2020/06/11/pasco-pta-zoom-meeting-gets-hacked-with-porn-racist-rants/

---

[16] Check Point 12 May 2020 - Coronavirus cyber-attacks update: beware of the phish: https://blog.checkpoint.com/security/coronavirus-cyber-attacks-update-beware-of-the-phish/

[17] Computer Weekly 3 August 2016 - One in five businesses hit by ransomware are forced to close, study shows: https://www.computerweekly.com/news/450301845/One-in-five-businesses-hit-by-ransomware-are-forced-to-close-study-shows

[18] Harvard Business Review 16 March 2020 - 15 Questions About Remote Work, Answered: https://hbr.org/2020/03/15-questions-about-remote-work-answered

[19] Conosco 21 December 2020 - 10 Undeniable Reasons Why Data Backup is so Important: https://conosco.com/industry-insights/blog/10-undeniable-reasons-why-data-backup-is-so-important

[20] GDPR Buzz 24 July 2018 - More than 40% of reported security breaches are caused by employee negligence: https://gdprbuzz.com/news/more-than-40-of-reported-security-breaches-are-caused-by-employee-negligence/

[21] Fox News 25 April 2020 - 10 COVID-19 scams spreading right now that people are falling for: https://www.foxnews.com/tech/10-covid-19-scams-spreading-right-now-that-people-are-falling-for

Printed in Great Britain
by Amazon

32274934R10106